Guided Meditation
and
Bedtime Stories for Kids

A Collection of Short Tales to
Help Children Relax, Learn Mindfulness
and Fall Asleep Faster

Ava Johansson

Copyright and Disclosures

Copyright © 2021 – by Mango Broom Ltd

All rights reserved. No part of this publication may be reproduced, distributed, or transmitted in any form or by any means, including photocopying, recording, or other electronic or mechanical methods without the prior written permission of the publisher, except in the case of brief quotations embodied in reviews and certain other noncommercial uses permitted by copyright law. For permission requests, please contact the publisher at the email address below.

Mango Broom Ltd
Email: sparkle@mangobroom.com
ISBN 9781913937027 (eBook)
ISBN 9781913937034 (print book)
First Edition

Legal and Disclaimer.

Please note the information contained within this book is for educational and entertainment purposes only.

Furthermore, the information contained in this book and its contents is not designed to replace or take the place of any form of medical, psychological, or professional advice; and it is not meant to replace the need for independent medical, financial, legal, or other professional advice or services as may be required. The content and information in this book have been provided for educational and entertainment purposes only.

The content and information contained in this book have been compiled from sources deemed reliable, and it is accurate to the best of the Publisher's and Author's knowledge, information, and belief. However, the Publisher or Author cannot guarantee its accuracy and validity and cannot be held liable for any errors and/or omissions. Further, changes are periodically made to this book as and when needed. Where appropriate and/or necessary, you must consult a professional (including but not limited to your doctor, attorney, financial advisor, or such other professional advisor) before using any of the suggested remedies, techniques, or information in this book.

Upon using the contents and information contained in this book, you agree to hold harmless the Publisher and Author from and against any damages, costs, and expenses, including any legal fees potentially resulting from the application of any information provided in this book. This disclaimer applies to any loss, damages, or injury caused by the use and application, whether directly or indirectly, of any advice or information presented, whether for breach of contract, tort, negligence, personal injury, criminal intent, or under any other cause of action.

You agree to accept all risks of using the information presented inside this book.

You agree by continuing to read this book that, where appropriate and/or necessary, you shall consult a professional (including but not limited to your doctor, attorney, financial advisor, or other such professional advisors) before using any of the suggested remedies, techniques, or information in this book. Reading the information in this book does not create a physician-patient relationship.

While many experiences related in this book are true, names and identifying details have been changed to protect the privacy of individuals.

YOUR FREE BONUS
The Beginners Guide to Mudras for Kids!

As a way of thanking you for your purchase, I have a **free bonus** to offer you.

Besides the beautiful meditation and bedtime stories provided in this book, I have created **The Beginners Guide to Mudras for Kids,** which will teach your kids the hand symbols they can use during a guided meditation story. The guide explains why mudras are beneficial and what it all means. Your kids will master the main mudras in no time.

Click (or tap) below to get your FREE Bonus instantly.

Click here:
https://www.mangobroom.com/mudras-kids/

Contents

Introduction 1
Story 1: A Day at the Enchanted Beach 11
Story 2: A Wander in a Magical Rainforest 19
Story 3: Dreamland 25
Story 4: Flower Fields 31
Story 5: Relaxing on a Cloud 37
Story 6: Super Senses 43
Story 7: Rainbow Slide 51
Story 8: Floating in Space 57
Story 9: Zoo Adventure 63
Story 10: Fruitland 69
Story 11: Talking Teddy Bears 75
Story 12: Art World 81
Story 13: The Friendly Pirates 91
Story 14: The Grand Dance of the Seahorses 99
Story 15: The Dog Park 105
Story 16: Snow Globe 111
Story 17: The Magic Sandpit 119
Story 18: The Enchanting Garden 125
Story 19: Camping in the Wild 131
Story 20: Superhero Party 137
Conclusion 145
References 153

Introduction

Children are born with a natural curiosity and excitement for life. They find joy in the small moments, often pointing out little details to adults that perhaps we hadn't noticed or had forgotten to see.

A child may comment on the way a butterfly flaps its wings or the vibrant color of a ladybug. They may shriek with delight when touching a soft, fluffy cat or widen their eyes when seeing a giraffe for the first time. Often, children can be our greatest teachers, encouraging us to be in the moment and join them in taking in its wonder and joy.

However, in this dynamic, fastpaced, and ever-changing world, children's brains can become overstimulated, resulting in fatigue. The higher stress levels found in children these days can contribute to exhausted minds.

To combat the weariness and help kids to unwind and switch off, meditation is a tool that can be used to improve their clarity, help them gain confidence, and stimulate a better overall sense of wellbeing.

According to Head Space, meditation is about

listening to your feelings and emotions and just letting them be. The overall aim is to be able to learn to understand yourself better and become comfortable with who you are and how your mind works.

It isn't about trying to become a "better" person, but more about learning to tap into a sense of mindfulness that enables you to look at and handle situations positively.

Yoga International states: "When you meditate, you give yourself an inner vacation." If your child can master or at least practice meditation and learn to go within, this can be a very powerful tool for them, one that they will carry through to adulthood.

Why is Meditation for Children Beneficial?

Meditation for children offers countless mental and physical benefits. When the mind slows down and focus and attention are turned inward and toward the breathing, the central nervous system also slows down, allowing a child's body to relax.

A relaxed body decreases levels of stress and anxiety and allows for a night of deeper sleep, which in turn is beneficial for every aspect of their lives, especially in those crucial developmental years.

Children that practice meditation improve their level of imagination and often become more resourceful. Additionally, their attention span improves, and many children develop an increased sense of awareness.

A study was conducted by *Pediatrics*, the Official

Journal of the American Academy of Pediatrics, on a group of three hundred middleschool children who came from lowincome backgrounds. It found that mindful meditation was able to improve psychological functioning and decrease levels of posttraumatic stress disorder (PTSD) in the children.

Another study was conducted on a group of teenagers who were at risk of developing cardiovascular disease. They were taught mindfulness, breathing, and meditation, and the study found that their blood pressure and heart rates decreased.

There is also evidence that meditation can soothe gastrointestinal disorders and reduce obesity, high blood pressure, headaches, and pain sensitivity, as well as boost immune function.

A group of Harvard neuroscientists ran an eight-week study on people who practiced meditation every day. The results concluded that there was an increase in gray matter in their brains, as well as a heightened sense of empathy and creativity, and better sleep patterns.

This is no different with children. Dr. Bryan Bruno, founder and Medical Director at MidCity TMS New York, says that "meditation is one of the healthiest activities that a parent can do with their child." He believes that meditation has a direct, positive effect on the parietal lobe in the brain, which slows down when a person is meditating. This means a child engaging in meditation can understand the world around them more clearly.

Mindfulness vs. Meditation

While mindfulness and meditation often overlap and share similar traits, they do differ. But most importantly, they are both beneficial for children.

Mindfulness trains the mind to respond "mindfully" to what is going on around the body. For example, a child is playing in the playground at school and another student accidentally steps on their toe. In general, most children would cry and blame the other child for hurting them.

However, a child that practices mindfulness regularly would most likely look at that situation differently. They wouldn't react straight away and would realize that the other child didn't hurt them intentionally. They would perhaps ask the other child to be careful.

Jon KabatZinn, an American professor emeritus of medicine and the creator of the Stress Reduction Clinic and the Center for Mindfulness in Medicine, Health Care, and Society at the University of Massachusetts Medical School defines mindfulness as "paying attention in a particular way, on purpose, in the present moment and nonjudgmentally."

The main difference between meditation and mindfulness is that meditation can be considered as more of an activity for the mind, whereas mindfulness requires the mind to merely observe.

However, both can be done together. For example, a child can be taught to eat mindfully. They can slow down their chewing, tasting each bite and feeling the texture of the food in their mouth. This is the mindful part. But the feeling of calm and the way the child feels inside is part of meditation.

Guided Meditation Before Bed

Guided meditations for children work very well to send them off into a deep and peaceful sleep. Meditation expert, hypnotherapist, and author Cory Cochiolo encourages including guided meditations as part of your child's bedtime routine. She thinks doing so makes it a positive experience in which a child feels warm, safe, happy, and comfortable.

This Book

The purpose of this book is to help your child cultivate their inner calm. The twenty stories are designed to take your child into a meditative and mindful state, at their level, in a fun, playful, and gentle way. Some of the stories include everyday settings, while others focus on fantasy.

The book aims to stimulate your child's imagination while teaching them the art of meditation and mindfulness. The stories are designed to be read before bed to ensure a deep and restful sleep, but they can also be read during the daytime. Guided meditations for children during the day are an excellent way of refocusing their minds, allowing them to be more productive and creative throughout the rest of their day. Whenever a parent wants to practice guided meditation and mindfulness with their child, this book is here for that purpose.

Getting Started

You can start reading guided meditations to your child at any age – the earlier, the better. Meditation and mindfulness practice with your child can take place anywhere, at any time, although certain factors make for a more conducive atmosphere.

Voice

A smooth, soothing voice when reading bedtime meditations to your child is crucial. Throughout the stories, there are places where you can pause, pace your words, or perhaps make your voice a little quieter. The way you speak will set the tone for the story and your child's body will respond accordingly. Along the way, watch how your child reacts to your tone, and notice when their bodies relax more.

It is helpful to practice the tone of voice you will use when reading before you start, and the more you read to them in this way the more they will become used to it and associate it with a positive, relaxing experience.

Surroundings

Simply put, the more comfortable your child, the better. If you are reading to your child before bed, then their bedroom is the best place to do so. Make sure they are lying down, warm and cozy in their bed, perhaps with their favorite blanket, pillow, or stuffed toy with them if that is something they want.

They should do their bedtime routine, such as baths and brushing their teeth, before the guided meditations, so they don't need to get out of bed when you finish. The environment should be quiet and peaceful, especially if your child nods off to sleep during the story.

If you are reading to them during the day, your child can sit on a chair or couch, or simply lie flat on the floor, perhaps on a yoga mat. Remember, these stories aren't there just to induce sleep, but to make your child feel calm and relaxed.

It is a good idea to designate a certain space in your house for reading during the day. You will find the storyreading to be less successful if you are in a noisy or peoplepacked environment. The quiet helps your child focus better.

Checkin

Before you start the guided meditations, it is a good idea to check in with your child. Ask them if they have any worries so you can talk about them before you start. You want your child to be clearheaded when meditating, so they can take it all in and make the most out of the experience.

Perhaps you can check in with your child a few hours before the guided meditation, so they have time to download and process any thoughts or feelings they have, or perhaps you may make it an evening ritual during bath time to ask them how they are feeling.

Music

Perhaps your child loves soothing, peaceful music playing in the background. That is fine, as long as it doesn't distract from the guided meditation. Calming music is a great way to relax your child and help send them off to sleep. This is also useful because they can play this music by themselves when you are not around to read to them.

Breathing

Before the guided meditation or story starts, find a still moment with your child and ask them to concentrate on their breath. You can ask them to place a hand on their belly and take five deep breaths in and out. They can feel the rise and fall of their belly with their hand, and this helps them settle into a feeling of calm and focus before you start reading to them.

Another breathing technique that works well with children is counting. Ask them to breathe in, counting 1, 2, 3, 4, and then to breathe out, counting 1, 2, 3, 4, taking a pause when they have emptied their lungs. Children tend to remember this way of breathing and can even use it in daytoday life to calm themselves if they are feeling stressed or overwhelmed.

Hand Movements

Positioning the hands in one of various poses is called a "mudra." It is a symbol, made with the hands, that locks and stores energy within the body. Teaching children mudras gives them a skill they can keep for life; research shows that mudras activate a part of a child's brain that generates a brainbody connection. This feeling of aligning the mind with the body has positive effects on a child, inducing focus, calmness, and awareness.

There are many different types of mudras a child can make. A popular and common one to use while meditating is the "Gyan" mudra. This pose is done by touching your index fingertip to the tip of your thumb while holding the other three fingers out straight. This mudra invites concentration and focus.

Another popular mudra is "Namaste hands." This involves holding your hands together in prayer position at your heart. This mudra invites balance.

Children often have fun learning different mudras and this can be incorporated into the guided meditations.

STORY 1
A Day at the Enchanted Beach

Getting Comfy

Settle into a cozy and comfortable position. Take a deep breath in, slowly filling up your lungs with air, and then let it all out with a sigh. Feel your body sinking deeper into the bed *(or couch)* and relax your head. If it feels good for you, close your eyes.

Simply listen to the sound of my voice and let your mind drift away.

Think about your little body, lying still and feeling warm. You can feel your chest rising and falling with each breath you take. Think about your feet and ten toes. Maybe your feet are falling out to the side. Maybe they are pointing straight up. However they are positioned is perfect.

Think about your hands and ten fingers. Perhaps your hands are resting next to you or gently resting on

your belly. (*Mention mudras only if your child practices them*).

Think about your mouth, your nose, your eyes. Relax them, letting the mouth fall open or stay closed, whichever is comfortable, and let the eyelids grow heavy and fall shut.

You feel completely relaxed, calm, and peaceful. You are safe. You are very loved.

Guided Meditation Story

I want you to imagine that you are on the beach. Your family has taken a lovely little trip to the beach for the day. However, it is not just any kind of beach. It is an enchanted beach.

As soon as you arrive at the beach, you can feel the wind dancing through your hair, and you can smell the salt in the air.

You close your eyes and take a deep breath so you can smell the salt even more. You can smell the fresh ocean, the sand, and maybe you even catch a little whiff of ice cream on the breeze. It smells exactly like your favorite flavor of ice cream.

When you open your eyes, you can see the warm white sand in front of you and the bright blue ocean stretching out as far as the eye can see. You and your family start to walk down to the beach, and when you reach the sand it feels warm underneath your feet. You can feel your toes squishing...and squishing...and squishing into the sand.

Story 1: A Day at the Enchanted Beach

It feels nice and tickles a little. You turn your face up to the sky. You can feel the warm sunshine on your face. It warms up your cheeks, your nose, and your forehead. You lay out your brightly colored towel on the sand and slowly sink onto it. You can feel the sand under the towel. It is very soft, everything is peaceful as the wind whispers across the ocean shores.

You stand up and make your way down toward the ocean. The water is calm and still and there are no waves in sight.

As you stand on the shoreline, you notice that the water looks like a glittering mirror. Every time you move your head, the water sparkles. It is so beautiful.

In the distance, you see a shimmering tail. Is that the tail of a fish? You look closer and you can see that the tail is green, as it comes to the surface and playfully dips back under the water. You rub your eyes and look again. Wow, you think. It looks like a mermaid!

You approach the shoreline and dip your toes into the water. It is slightly warm, so you decide to go in even further. The sun feels heavenly as it beams down on your shoulders. You slowly glide into the ocean until the water reaches your waist.

The tail is coming closer, and suddenly, with a splash of water, a mermaid does a backflip right in front of you! She dives back down into the water and swims up to you. She is very pretty. She has long, flowing, brown hair, and on her ears, she wears little shell-shaped earrings.

"Hi! I'm Mary the Mermaid!" says the mermaid, as

she does another backflip. She has very good swimming skills – you wish you could swim like Mary. You tell her your name and she asks if this is your first time to the enchanted beach. You say it is, and that you would love to be able to swim as fast as her and be able to breathe underwater, too.

Mary pulls a pair of flippers and a snorkel from out of the water. She says, "Here, put these on!" Where did they come from!? This really *is* an enchanted beach. You carefully put your flippers on your feet and adjust your snorkel in place.

You glide out deeper into the ocean, kicking your feet behind you. Your flippers make you go extra fast. Mary tells you to follow her.

Dipping your head under the water, you open your eyes and are amazed at what you see. Bright, colorful fish are swimming everywhere. Red, blue, pink, orange – it looks like a rainbow right before your eyes. There are fish of all shapes and sizes. Big, small, fat, thin, round. Some have stripes, others have spots.

Mary is smoothly swimming through the water in front of you. She signals to you to keep following her. You continue swimming, noticing the incredible blue and green coral underneath you.

Finally, Mary stops and tells you to wait. You stay on the surface of the water, bobbing up and down as you peer under the water. You can see her green, shimmering tail heading deeper and deeper until you can no longer see her.

You wait for Mary to return while you gaze around

at this wonderful underwater world. You realize how much life we cannot see goes on under the ocean. You feel lucky that you can peek into the lives of these underwater creatures.

After a few moments, you see Mary swimming back up, with something in her hand. She reaches the surface and sticks her head out of the water. She stretches out her hand and opens it up.

Resting in her hand is a small, shiny, delicate pearl. "This is for you," says Mary. "Whenever you feel worried, or scared, or alone, hold this pearl in your hand and you will feel better." She places the pearl in your hand. It feels cool and smooth.

As you hold the pearl, it starts to glow. It starts to feel warm and you wrap your fingers around it. You close your eyes, feeling the glow. It feels lovely. You feel good and you know that whenever you think about the pearl, you will feel calm, no matter what.

You thank Mary for the gift. She grins and tells you that there is an octopus a few miles away who needs her help, and with a flip of her tail, she disappears back into the big, wide, peaceful ocean.

Gently, you lie back into the water, so you are flat on your back, floating. It feels like you are lying on a cloud. You can hear the sound of your gentle breathing as you look up at the sky. It is bright and blue...and heavenly.

Time passes as you lay floating, feeling as light as a feather. All your worries melt away. You don't have a care in the world. You feel safe, relaxed, and lovely.

Your eyes are closed, and you can feel the rays from the sun melting onto your eyelids.

In the distance, you begin to hear a soft, familiar melody. It tickles your ears. It sounds like the icecream van! Slowly, you flip off your back and look into the distance, toward the beach. You see a bright pink van with a giant icecream cone on top. Your family is calling you over, smiling. They know that ice cream is one of your favorite treats.

You make your way back onto the sand and start to skip towards the icecream van. When you get there, you can feel the icy, cool blast of air coming from inside the van. Your mom asks which flavor you want, and you look down at the brightly colored icecream tubs. There are a lot of choices. You tell the man you want an ice cream that a mermaid would like.

The icecream man smiles and winks at you. He picks up a waffle cone shaped like a fish and fills it with an aquacolored scoop, a lightpinkcolored scoop, and a goldencolored scoop. Golden ice cream!? Oh, boy, you have never had golden ice cream before.

The icecream man hands you your special mermaid ice cream. You lick the aquacolored scoop first; it tastes just like bubble gum! Next, you take a lick of the lightpinkcolored scoop; it tastes like fairy floss! Finally, you lick the goldencolored scoop; it tastes like all your favorite sweets combined. Delicious! You walk with your ice cream back down to the sand and sit down on your towel.

The sun is starting to set, and it is time to say

goodbye to the enchanted beach. You have had a lovely day and you are feeling sleepy from your adventures. You fall asleep in the car on the way home, and when you arrive your mom picks you up and carries you to your bed. She tucks you in, kisses you on the forehead, and wishes you a peaceful sleep full of beautiful dreams.

STORY 2
A Wander in a Magical Rainforest

Getting Comfy

Settle into a cozy and comfortable position. Take a deep breath in, slowly filling up your lungs with air, and then let it all out with a sigh. Feel your body sinking deeper into the bed (*or couch*) and relax your head. If it feels good for you, close your eyes.

Simply listen to the sound of my voice and let your mind drift away.

Think about your little body, lying still and feeling warm. You can feel your chest rising and falling with each breath you take. Think about your feet and ten toes. Maybe your feet are falling out to the side. Maybe they are pointing straight up. However they are positioned is perfect.

Think about your hands and ten fingers. Perhaps your hands are resting next to you or gently resting on

your belly. (*Mention mudras only if your child practices them*).

Think about your mouth, your nose, your eyes. Relax them, letting the mouth fall open or stay closed, whichever is comfortable, and let the eyelids grow heavy and fall shut.

You feel completely relaxed, calm, and peaceful. You are safe. You are very loved.

Guided Meditation Story

Today, you are going for a wander through a lush rainforest. You arrive at the entrance of the rainforest. Sounds of birds calling out, insects humming, and a waterfall in the distance are all around you. The air is cool and damp, and the temperature is perfect.

You take a deep breath and smell the scent of the forest in front of you. It smells like sweet flowers and earth. It curls up through your nostrils and in through your lungs. The air is pure, and it feels good to slowly breathe it in, through your nose, and out, through your nose.

You see a path on the ground, covered in leaves, and you start to follow it into the rainforest. As you walk, you can see all the small, friendly insects of the forest scuttling around, busily building their homes with twigs and little stones. The forest is alive with life.

Up ahead, you can see a group of bright red mushrooms with white spots. They look so lovely and remind you of the fairy tales that have been read to you. And, what's that you see sitting behind one of the mushrooms? With his red cap, white beard, and blue little cardigan, it looks like a dwarf! He is sleeping, snoring softly.

He looks so relaxed and peaceful, you don't want to disturb him. Very quietly, like a mouse, you start to creep past him. But just as you are nearly out of sight, you hear him wake up. You turn around and the sweet dwarf is looking right at you.

"Hello there!" he calls. "Hello!" you say back. "I am the calmest dwarf in the whole forest. My name is Mr. Unflappable, because nothing gets me into a flap!" says the dwarf.

You introduce yourself and tell him that you are going for a wander through the forest. "Good idea," says Mr. Unflappable. "This forest is the most peaceful place in the world. Walking through here makes you slow down. Your breath, your heartbeat, even the way you walk. It is very soothing".

You tell him that you noticed that and that since you have entered the forest, you are feeling light, happy, and perhaps even a little sleepy. Mr. Unflappable nods his head and tells you that is how everyone feels when they walk through this magical forest. He tells you to look up at the tall tree behind him.

The tree has a thick, sturdy trunk and you look all the way up the top of the tree. Its branches are long, and its leaves are dark green, sprouting out in all directions. Through the top of the tree, there is a small opening. You can see a bit of beautiful, blue sky, and the sun is beaming down through the opening.

As you continue to look up, Mr. Unflappable asks you to describe what you are feeling. You tell him that the sun's rays are falling onto your face, warming up your entire body. Your forehead, your nose, your mouth, your cheeks, your neck, your shoulders, your arms, your hands, and your fingers. You tell him that you can feel this warm glow spreading down to your chest, your belly, your legs, your feet, and your toes.

"It is a lovely feeling, isn't it?" Mr. Unflappable asks. You nod your head in agreement. "Stay in this moment and enjoy how it feels. You are warm, calm, safe and everything is okay" says Mr. Unflappable. You savor the moment, soaking in the warmth of the sun's rays.

After a few minutes, you hear Mr. Unflappable greeting someone else. "Well, hello there, Mrs. Flutterby!" you hear him say. You turn around and see the most magnificent, brightly colored butterfly floating toward you. She has orange, purple, and blue wings which she flaps gently and gracefully.

You reach your hand out, hypnotized by her beauty, and the butterfly smoothly flies over to you and perches herself on your hand. "This is Mrs. Flutterby" chimes in Mr. Unflappable. "She is the most beautiful butterfly in all the forest".

Mrs. Flutterby flaps her wings and her eyelashes as her way of greeting you. You are mesmerized by her beauty and elegance. Mr. Unflappable tells you that Mrs. Flutterby is very good at keeping secrets and that if there is anything at all on your mind that you want to tell her, you can whisper into her ear.

Story 2: A Wander in a Magical Rainforest

You have a little think. Some thoughts come to your mind and you lean down and whisper them into Mrs. Flutterby's ear. She flaps her wings in response. Then, you notice that your chest feels lighter. You feel like a little weight has been lifted from your shoulders. You feel fantastic.

You tell Mr. Unflappable how you feel, and he says that this is a normal and positive feeling. He explains that by sharing your thoughts with Mrs. Flutterby, you have been able to let go of any tension that you were holding.

You thank Mrs. Flutterby for being so trusting by giving her a butterfly kiss! You flutter your eyelashes against hers. It tickles and makes you giggle. Mrs. Flutterby spreads open her wings and gently glides off into the air. You watch her vibrant colors disappear into the forest.

Mr. Unflappable holds out his hand. You take his hand and the two of you continue along the path, through the forest together. You chat about all sorts of things and you laugh a lot too – Mr. Unflappable is very funny!

After a lovely stroll, you finally reach the end of the path, where you see your mom, waiting for you with outstretched arms, ready to take you back home.

You turn to Mr. Unflappable and thank him for the walk, the great chat, and all the giggles. "You're welcome. When you get back home, you will probably feel sleepy. So, if it is bedtime, you can hop into your nice, warm, cozy bed. Before you fall asleep, take some last deep breaths, in and out, and I hope you will doze off and enjoy beautiful dreams" says Mr. Unflappable.

You smile from cheek to cheek, wave goodbye, and run into your mom's arms. She gives you a giant hug, squeezing you tight, telling you how she missed you while you were on your adventure.

You turn around to take a photograph in your mind of the magical forest, and in the distance, through the trees, you can see the glimmer of brightly colored butterfly wings. You smile to yourself.

Your mom takes your hand in hers and the two of you head off home. It has been a big day and you cannot wait to crawl into your comfy bed with all your pillows and stuffed animals and fall off into a deep and peaceful slumber.

STORY 3
Dreamland

Getting Comfy

Settle into a cozy and comfortable position. Take a deep breath in, slowly filling up your lungs with air, and then let it all out with a sigh. Feel your body sinking deeper into the bed (*or couch*) and relax your head. If it feels good for you, close your eyes.

Simply listen to the sound of my voice and let your mind drift away.

Think about your little body, lying still and feeling warm. You can feel your chest rising and falling with each breath you take. Think about your feet and ten toes. Maybe your feet are falling out to the side. Maybe they are pointing straight up. However they are positioned is perfect.

Think about your hands and ten fingers. Perhaps your hands are resting next to you or gently resting on your belly. (*Mention mudras only if your child practices them*).

Think about your mouth, your nose, your eyes. Relax them, letting the mouth fall open or stay closed, whichever is comfortable, and let the eyelids grow heavy and fall shut.

You feel completely relaxed, calm, and peaceful. You are safe. You are very loved.

Guided Meditation Story

Today, you are feeling sleepy. So sleepy that it is the perfect time to nod off and have a wonderful dream. Your body is feeling heavy and your eyes want to close. There is magic waiting for you as soon as you fall asleep. So, when you're ready, let your body completely relax and enter into dreamland.

Well done! You're in. Dreamland is a beautiful place. As you look around, you are amazed by what you see. Everything is so bright, shiny, and colorful. The grass you are standing on is a deep green and feels soft as silk underneath your bare feet. You look up at the sky, which is a dazzling blue.

All around you are tiny little fairies with wings. You can hear their wings flapping rapidly; they make a humming noise. The fairies are only the size of your hand and are adorable!

It looks like they are all busy preparing something. You look closer. They are making a big glass of watermelon lemonade, and what looks like your favorite cookies!

One of the tiny fairies signals you to sit down, so you do. You lower yourself onto the soft, wispy grass and take a seat, with your legs crossed. After a moment, a group of fairies pick up the glass and the plate with the cookies and flutter them over to you. They place them gently on the ground in front of you.

You thank the sweet fairies and give them your biggest smile. You pick up the glass and take a sip. Ahh, watermelon lemonade! So refreshing. You reach for one of the cookies and take a bite. It is delicious; it tastes like chocolate, vanilla, and sprinkles. As you continue to drink your lemonade, you notice how calm you are feeling.

Your breath is soft, and your chest feels light. Your shoulders are relaxed, and you feel content and happy that you are in Dreamland, a place that is safe, peaceful, and always ready to welcome you in. A place where butterflies float and fairies fly and even the raindrops are coated in candy.

In the distance, you see something glittering, moving. As it starts to get closer, you realize that it is…a unicorn! It has a beautiful, big, white, sturdy body with a pink and purple mane, purple hooves, and a stunning silverandgold horn.

You can't believe it! You have heard of unicorns before, but you have never actually seen one. You watch as the gentle beast slowly makes its way over to you. "Hello!" you call when the unicorn arrives. "Why, hello!" says the unicorn. "I'm Nigel, the one and only unicorn in Dreamland; nice to meet you."

You stand up as he offers you a hoof to shake. "Nice

to meet you, Nigel! I am currently in the middle of having a dream," you say.

"Yes, you are! And what a pleasant dream you are having. Please, sit back down, enjoy your lemonade". You plop back down onto the grass and Nigel joins you. He lays on his side and stretches out.

"The watermelon lemonade you're drinking is magic," says Nigel. "It makes you feel relaxed." You smile, nodding, and tell him you noticed how relaxed you felt. Nigel notices you staring at his horn. "Stare all you want, I don't mind. I know how beautiful it is" Nigel says, with a laugh that sounds like bells.

"It *is* beautiful," you say. "What does your horn do?"

"Oh, many wonderful things, my friend. One of the best things it does is grant wishes" replies Nigel. Your eyes grow wide. "Grant wishes?" you repeat. "Yes! One wish per person, anything you want" offers Nigel.

Wow! Nigel really is a magical unicorn. You start to think about all the things you wish for most in the world. A giant bar of chocolate. Or a puppy or kitten to have as your own. Maybe even a beach in your yard at home. "I know!" you say. "I would like to fly."

Nigel smiles. "Very well, your wish is my command." He blinks three times, and his horn turns from silver and gold to a glowing orange color. "Enjoy!" calls out Nigel, as your body starts to float off the ground. You float higher, looking down at Nigel and the fairies below. You spread out your arms and discover that they are your wings.

Story 3: Dreamland

You turn to the right and soar out into the blue sky. The wind whips through your hair. "Weeeeeeeeeee!" you cry. What an amazing feeling! You feel as light as a feather, as you fly across the sky. You dip and twirl, spin and flip. You look down at everything beneath you. Nigel's horn is a tiny, glowing orange dot.

As you continue to fly, you notice the air begins to change color. It goes from blue to a dusky pink. The sun is beginning to set here in Dreamland, and from high in the air, you can see the most beautiful sunset you've ever seen in your whole life. You stop for a moment, hovering in the sky as you watch the sun slowly setting. You can feel the warmth from the sun as it passes you by and begins to retire for the night.

What a perfect dream this has turned out to be! Very gently, you start to lower back down to the grass. Slowly, Nigel and the fairies start to become clearer as you come closer to the ground. They all start clapping, applauding you, and when your feet hit the earth, you take a little bow.

"Bravo! Well done. Was that your first time flying?" asks Nigel. You tell him it was. "I am impressed! You are a master flyer. You will have to come back to Dreamland soon and try it again."

Nigel pulls a flute out from his mane and brings it to his lips. When he blows into the flute, the loveliest melody floats out. You have never heard music like this before.

The fairies all stop what they are doing and flutter down onto the grass around you and Nigel. They are mesmerized. They close their eyes and start to sway from side to side. The melody is so soothing, so soft, you also close your eyes. You begin to drift off.

When you open your eyes, you find yourself back in your bed, in your bedroom. Your blanket is tucked in around you and you feel warm and cozy. What a brilliant dream, you think. And you close your eyes once again, ready to begin your next adventure.

STORY 4
Flower Fields

Getting Comfy

Settle into a cozy and comfortable position. Take a deep breath in, slowly filling up your lungs with air, and then let it all out with a sigh. Feel your body sinking deeper into the bed (*or couch*) and relax your head. If it feels good for you, close your eyes.

Simply listen to the sound of my voice and let your mind drift away.

Think about your little body, lying still and feeling warm. You can feel your chest rising and falling with each breath you take. Think about your feet and ten toes. Maybe your feet are falling out to the side. Maybe they are pointing straight up. However they are positioned is perfect.

Think about your hands and ten fingers. Perhaps your hands are resting next to you or gently resting on your belly. (*Mention mudras only if your child practices them*).

Think about your mouth, your nose, your eyes. Relax them, letting the mouth fall open or stay closed, whichever is comfortable, and let the eyelids grow heavy and fall shut.

You feel completely relaxed, calm, and peaceful. You are safe. You are very loved.

Guided Meditation Story

Today you find yourself in a field full of flowers. Everywhere you look are gorgeous flowers. Big, small, starshaped, round, tall, short. The colors are like a rainbow. Reds, oranges, yellows, greens, blues, indigos, and violets.

You take the biggest breath that you have taken all day. You can smell the sweet scent of flowers blooming. It whistles up your nostrils and fills your nose with a melting pot of floral aroma. Stretching out your hands, you touch the delicate petals of a deep blue flower. The petals feel like velvet between your fingers.

You are enjoying your time, wandering around from flower to flower, taking in everything you see, smell, and feel. Suddenly, you hear a soft buzzing noise in the distance. You glance up and see a large, elegant, blackandyellow bee flying towards you. The bee is wearing a golden crown and carrying a golden staff.

Bzzz! Bzzz! The bee stops in front of you. "Oh, hello! Allow me to introduce myself. I am Queen Bee" says the bee as she bats her eyelashes. You say hello and find yourself giving her a little bow. Isn't that what you do when you meet royalty?! Queen Bee bats her eyelashes again. "Oh darling, you're sweet, like honey. And speaking of honey, I need your help".

Paying attention, you listen to Queen Bee's request for help. "I am looking for the biggest, most beautiful flowers in these fields so I can drink the nectar to make honey. Will you help me search for the perfect flowers?" asks Queen Bee. Of course, you will, you tell her; in fact, you would be delighted to, you love flowers!

Queen Bee thanks you and asks you to climb on her back. "It's much quicker this way" explains Queen Bee. She rolls out a little step ladder and up you climb, securing yourself onto Queen Bee's back and holding onto her soft fluffy body. "Ready?" she asks. "Ready!" you say.

Queen Bee spreads her delicate wings and up, up, and away you both fly! Buzz! Buzz! You look down below and can see the tops of all the colorful flowers. "Let me know when you can see the perfect flower" calls out Queen Bee. As she continues to fly, circling around the flower fields, you see a tall, yellow flower. You point it out and Queen Bee flies down to it.

You hop off her back and go over to the flower. It has a dark center and large, beautiful yellow petals. "Good choice! This is a sunflower" says Queen Bee. "Not only is it perfect for pollinating, but in the spiritual world a sunflower symbolizes happiness and positivity." Queen Bee encourages you to touch the flower.

As you gently stroke the petals, you feel a wave of happiness and positivity sweep over your body. You feel light and cheerful, and when you think about the future you feel hopeful. Queen Bee flies toward the center of the sunflower and starts drinking the sweet nectar. When she is finished, you climb onto her back and continue your search.

In the air, you spot a bush with purple flowers. "That looks good!" you tell Queen Bee. You both swoop down toward the bush. When you arrive, you can smell a purpledelicious fragrance. "Ah, yes! Lavender. Another good choice!" says Queen Bee. "The scent of lavender helps people feel calm, eases muscle tension, and relieves feelings of stress."

You move closer to the lavender bush so you can catch a stronger whiff of the beautiful smell. As you continue to inhale the smell of the lavender deeply, you do notice that your body is feeling limp and soft. Your jaw is feeling relaxed and your shoulders aren't hunched up near your ears. You feel calm and grounded. It feels nice.

Queen Bee gets to work on the lavender, and when she is done you climb onto her back once more. "Help find me one last flower, dear child," says Queen Bee.

A few moments later, you see a skinny stem with a bright red flower on the top. You point it out and down again you fly. "My favorite flower to drink from!" cries Queen Bee. "The poppy flower symbolizes sleep."

As you look at the delicate yet strong poppy flower and marvel at its piercing red color, you notice your eyes are starting to feel heavy. Your body is relaxed and right now, you could definitely flop down into your bed and fall asleep.

Story 4: Flower Fields

Queen Bee notices your drooping eyelids. "It looks like someone is getting sleeeeeepy! Let's get going. I am going to take you home and tuck you into bed." You climb onto Queen Bee's back one last time. As you hold onto her body, you snuggle down into her yellow and black fuzz. You can feel yourself drifting off, slowly.

The next time you open your eyes, you are back in your own bed. You are feeling warm and calm and your body feels completely relaxed. You turn your head and notice a little vase on your bedside table with some flowers in it. A sunflower, a couple of lavender flowers, and a tall red poppy. You smile and settle back into your pillow, ready to fall into a deep and restful sleep.

STORY 5
Relaxing on a Cloud

Getting Comfy

Settle into a cozy and comfortable position. Take a deep breath in, slowly filling up your lungs with air, and then let it all out with a sigh. Feel your body sinking deeper into the bed (*or couch*) and relax your head. If it feels good for you, close your eyes.

Simply listen to the sound of my voice and let your mind drift away.

Think about your little body, lying still and feeling warm. You can feel your chest rising and falling with each breath you take. Think about your feet and ten toes. Maybe your feet are falling out to the side. Maybe they are pointing straight up. However they are positioned is perfect.

Think about your hands and ten fingers. Perhaps your hands are resting next to you or gently resting on your belly. (*Mention mudras only if your child practices them*).

Think about your mouth, your nose, your eyes. Relax them, letting the mouth fall open or stay closed, whichever is comfortable, and let the eyelids grow heavy and fall shut.

You feel completely relaxed, calm, and peaceful. You are safe. You are very loved.

Guided Meditation Story

Today's journey is going to take you up, up, and away. All the way through the sky, above the treetops and buildings, and right onto a white, fluffy cloud.

You find yourself lounging on top of a cloud. It feels like a giant, squishy marshmallow as you sink into the cloud. Your body feels supported as you let go of any tension you may be feeling in your body. You feel light, as if your body has no weight and you are simply floating.

As you lie there, enjoying the peace, you start to hear the most wonderful sound; a harp. You can hear the strings of a harp being played and it is simply music to your ears. You raise your head to see who is playing this gorgeous music, and on the cloud next to you sits an angel, playing her harp.

Her eyes are closed, as she gently plucks the strings with her fingers. She is completely absorbed in the music, feeling it with her entire body. You watch in wonder, as the music makes you feel like you are in a trance. Your mind, body, and soul are all harmonious. Your breath is slow and relaxed.

When she is finished playing the song, the angel

looks at you and smiles. She is very pretty. She wears a white robe and has long, luscious hair, with a halo hovering around her head. Glorious white wings spread out from her back. "Hello, there. I am Gaia, your guardian angel."

"My guardian angel?" you ask. "Yes," responds Gaia. "I watch over you and make sure you are always protected". "That's so cool! I always wondered if I had a guardian angel," you say. Gaia smiles. "Well, now you know you do."

"I am there all the time, but especially during hard times," says Gaia. You think back to a time that you found challenging and difficult. You realize that even though you may have felt sad or angry, you got through it and felt better again. As if Gaia can read your mind, she smiles and says, "Yes, I was there during that tough time and helped you get through it".

Knowing that you have a guardian angel looking out for you makes you feel safe and relaxed. "How wonderful!" you tell Gaia. "Now, get settled even deeper into your cloud. We are going to play a game," says Gaia. This sounds like fun! You love to play games.

Gaia tells you that this game is going to test your sense of smell. She brings out a little pot of oil and asks you to smell it. You inhale the aroma; it smells lovely, however, you can't quite put your finger on the scent. "I'll give you a couple of clues," says Gaia. The smell itself comes from a yellowcolored fruit and it is part of the citrus family."

You think for a moment. Then it hits you. "Lemon!"

you say. Gaia smiles. "Yes, it's lemon. Now tell me, after smelling this lemon oil, how do you feel?" asks Gaia. You check in with how you are feeling. "I feel calm and happy," you tell Gaia. "Good! Lemon oil relieves feelings of stress and lifts your mood. If you are ever feeling sad, take a whiff of lemon oil."

"Next we have this oil," says Gaia, holding out another pot of oil. You lean in to smell it. How heavenly! It smells like a beautiful flower! But what flower is it, you ask yourself. Again, as if reading your mind, Gaia says, "The flower this oil comes from is famous for being given as a dozen and is the symbol of love."

You know what it is! "Rose oil!" you exclaim. "That's right," says Gaia. "And if you are ever feeling worried about anything, inhale the aroma of rose oil. It helps you stop worrying." You make a note of that in your mind as you notice that all your worries have vanished.

"Lastly, take a deep sniff of this oil," says Gaia as she holds out another little pot of oil in front of your nose. You inhale deeply. *Mmm, that smells good*, you think. Gaia hints, "Again, this is a fruit, also part of the citrus family." "Orange!" you say. "Very good," she answers, "You are excellent at this game. Orange oil is known to give you an energy boost, which is perfect for those days when you are feeling a little lazy."

Gaia is right! After smelling the orange oil, you feel like you are ready to go on a cloud hike! But the comfort of your cloud feels too good and you are too snug to think about getting up. "Our sense of smell is really important when it comes to calming ourselves," says

Gaia. "Actually, it has been proven that a smell can trigger a memory more than an image does."

"Think about what smells you enjoy." You think about all your favorite smells. The smell of your mom's perfume. The way your hair smells after it has been washed. The smell of freshly cut grass. The smell of warm, baked apple pie. "Mmm, those smells are good!" says Gaia, again reading your mind. "How do you feel when you think of those smells?" she asks.

"I feel happy. I feel nice and warm, and relaxed," you say. Gaia smiles. "I am glad I have taught you how to use your sense of smell to relax".

Suddenly, you smell a familiar scent on the breeze. It is a smell you can't quite put your finger on and explain, but it makes you have a longing for your bed. "Gaia," you say, "I can smell the special smell of my bedroom and my bed and all my teddies." "Then you must go, my child, back to your bedroom, into your bed, and into a deep and peaceful sleep," says Gaia.

And in the blink of an eye, you are back in your own bed, amongst your pillows and teddies, snuggled into your blanket. You take a deep breath in, inhaling the familiar smell of home, and drift off into a lovely sleep.

STORY 6
Super Senses

Getting Comfy

Settle into a cozy and comfortable position. Take a deep breath in, slowly filling up your lungs with air, and then let it all out with a sigh. Feel your body sinking deeper into the bed (*or couch*) and relax your head. If it feels good for you, close your eyes.

Simply listen to the sound of my voice and let your mind drift away.

Think about your little body, lying still and feeling warm. You can feel your chest rising and falling with each breath you take. Think about your feet and ten toes. Maybe your feet are falling out to the side. Maybe they are pointing straight up. However they are positioned is perfect.

Think about your hands and ten fingers. Perhaps your hands are resting next to you or gently resting on your belly. (*Mention mudras only if your child practices them*).

Think about your mouth, your nose, your eyes. Relax them, letting the mouth fall open or stay closed, whichever is comfortable, and let the eyelids grow heavy and fall shut.

You feel completely relaxed, calm, and peaceful. You are safe. You are very loved.

Guided Meditation Story

On today's journey, you find yourself outside, on the grass in the middle of a beautiful green park close to your house. The weather is warm, and you feel relaxed. You can hear birds singing and calling to each other. You notice the grass underneath you is soft, and you are enjoying just simply sitting and being still.

You close your eyes for a moment, face up to the sun. When you open them again, you notice something shiny and gold in the grass a few meters away from you. You stand up and walk over to the object. Upon closer inspection, you can see that it is a glass bottle of some sort. The bottom of the bottle is wide and becomes narrow up the top. It is tinged a purple color.

What an earth is this, you wonder. You pick it up and hold it in your hands. The glass feels cool against your skin. Turning it over, you peer through the glass. There is nothing inside, but suddenly, the bottle starts to warm up. How strange! You place it back down on the ground and take a step back.

The bottle is now glowing a bright purple color and smoke is starting to come out of the top of the bottle! As you watch, the bottle produces a last big puff of

Story 6: Super Senses

smoke, and a purple woman, half your size, appears on the grass next to the bottle. "Oh, thank you!" the woman says. She has beautiful, long black hair that falls gracefully down her shoulders. She is wearing a pretty skirt with pictures of flowers all over it and a white top. On her feet are goldcolored sandals.

"I have been stuck inside that bottle for too long! It feels good to be out in the world again! Though I was in the middle of a bit of gardening!" says the woman. You ask her what she means. "Oh, sorry, I should explain," says the woman with a kind smile. "I am a genie and I live inside that bottle. But sometimes, no one finds me for a while, and I end up staying in there for too long. Someone must be holding the bottle in order for me to come out."

"A genie like from Aladdin?" you ask. The genie smiles again. "Sort of! My name is Gina the Genie, and yes, I do grant wishes." Your mind starts doing backflips with excitement. She grants wishes! You immediately start thinking of all the things you want. New toys, a neverending supply of ice cream, a little kitten...

"Can I wish for anything?" you ask Gina the Genie. "I can grant you one wish, but it has to be a superpower." she replies, "Any superpower you like."

Wow! This is even more exciting! You can be a superhero! "I want to be able to help others with my superpower. Can I please have 'super senses' so I can hear, taste, smell, touch, and see even better?" you ask.

Gina the Genie nods her head. "What a splendid wish! Your wish is my command," she says, as she claps her hands three times. You stand still, waiting for your superpower to start working.

All of a sudden, you can hear the pitterpatter of ants' feet on the ground. You look down and, almost as if you have magnifying glasses for eyes, you can see a line of little ants carrying a tiny crumb of food along the grass.

You look over at Gina the Genie. "Wow!" you say. "This is amazing. I can even hear the ants on the ground!". "I know, pretty cool, huh!" says Gina the Genie. "Well, thanks for letting me out of the bottle; my work here is done, and I must get back to my gardening. Enjoy your new superpower, it will only last a day," she says as she waves goodbye and, with a puff of smoke, is gone.

You crouch down to the ground and spot the ants again. Pitterpatter, pitterpatter, as their tiny feet scurry along the ground. You look in the direction they are going and see a small ants' nest. *They must be carrying that crumb back to their nest to feed their babies*, you think. It will take them a while, though, and you don't want their babies to feel hungry.

Very gently, you place your hand out on the grass in front of the ants. They stop, squeaking among each other, and then, one by one, they lightly crawl onto your hand, bringing their crumb with them. You can feel the tiny little hairs on the bottom of their feet on your skin. It tickles a little. You have never felt anything like this before.

Once they are all safely on your palm, they stand

still. Very slowly, you stand up, and with a steady hand, you walk over to their nest, which is a few meters away.

When you get to the nest, you crouch down and place your hand on the ground. Just as the ants crawled onto your palm, one by one, they start to move off, one by one, dragging the crumb with them. You hear them squeaking at you as they rush into their nest, and think it must be their way of saying thankyou.

Mmm, what is that smell? On the breeze, you can faintly smell something delicious. You stand up, using your nose to follow the smell. The scent takes you out of the park, a few streets away, and into your house. You walk inside and into the kitchen. Your mom is standing over the stove, stirring a big pot.

"Oh! There you are!" says your mom. You tell her you smelled something delicious cooking, all the way from the park. She looks at you strangely. "Well, I am glad you are here because I need you to taste this pumpkin soup for me. My nose is blocked, and I can't taste anything," she says as she dips a spoon into the soup and holds it out to you.

You take the spoon and blow on the orangecolored soup to cool it down. You pop the spoon into your mouth. The warm soup melts in your mouth. It is very tasty. You can taste the ripe pumpkin, the velvety cream, and the fresh nutmeg. This is the most delicious thing you have ever tasted!

"Yum, mom! This soup is amazing!" you say. "Oh, good!" says your mom, "Then I don't need to add anything else to it and it's ready."

She gives the soup a final stir and asks you to sit down at the table for dinner. You enjoy a meal of pumpkin soup and buttered bread, followed by bright red strawberries dipped in milk chocolate.

With every bite you take, you can feel the crunch of the strawberries in your mouth and the sweetness of the chocolate on your tongue. Dessert has never tasted this good! These senses that Gina the Genie has given you are so much fun.

After dinner, you wash up, put on your pajamas, and hop into bed. Your sheets feel soft against your skin. The fur from your teddy bear tickles your cheek as you put your arm around him. Your mom comes into your bedroom to say goodnight. As she leans down to give you a big hug goodnight, you can smell her perfume on her neck. It wafts through your nostrils.

This is one of your favorite smells in the whole world. It simply smells like your mom. You wrap your arms around her. "I love you, have sweet dreams," she says. "I love you too, mom. I have had such a wonderful day" you say. She smiles at you and closes your door. What a big day you've had.

As you lie in your bed, cozy and warm, you can feel sleep is on its way. Your eyes are heavy and as you close them, you drift off into a world of genies and wishes.

YOUR FREE BONUS
The Beginners Guide to Mudras for Kids!

As a way of thanking you for your purchase, I have a **free bonus** to offer you.

Besides the beautiful meditation and bedtime stories provided in this book, I have created **The Beginners Guide to Mudras for Kids,** which will teach your kids the hand symbols they can use during a guided meditation story. The guide explains why mudras are beneficial and what it all means. Your kids will master the main mudras in no time.

Click (or tap) below to get your FREE Bonus instantly.

Click here:
https://www.mangobroom.com/mudras-kids/

STORY 7
Rainbow Slide

Getting Comfy

Settle into a cozy and comfortable position. Take a deep breath in, slowly filling up your lungs with air, and then let it all out with a sigh. Feel your body sinking deeper into the bed (*or couch*) and relax your head. If it feels good for you, close your eyes.

Simply listen to the sound of my voice and let your mind drift away.

Think about your little body, lying still and feeling warm. You can feel your chest rising and falling with each breath you take. Think about your feet and ten toes. Maybe your feet are falling out to the side. Maybe they are pointing straight up. However they are positioned is perfect.

Think about your hands and ten fingers. Perhaps your hands are resting next to you or gently resting on your belly. (*Mention mudras only if your child practices them*).

Think about your mouth, your nose, your eyes. Relax them, letting the mouth fall open or stay closed, whichever is comfortable, and let the eyelids grow heavy and fall shut.

You feel completely relaxed, calm, and peaceful. You are safe. You are very loved.

Guided Meditation Story

It's been a drizzly, wet morning and you've been inside, sitting at the window, watching the raindrops slide down the windowpane. There is a warm fire burning in the fireplace. Your cheeks are pink, and you feel warm and cozy as you sit watching the world outside.

The sound of the rain against the roof – pitterpatter, pitterpatter – makes you feel calm and sleepy. You love the sound it makes, especially when you are comfy and dry inside. You curl up where you are and drift off into a deep and delicious sleep.

The rain has stopped! The sun is shining, and guess what else is shining, high up in the sky? A rainbow! The outer layer of color is a bright red, the next layer is a dazzling orange, followed by a banana yellow, lime green, sky blue, ocean blue, and finally, a beautiful violet color.

You squeeze your eyes shut and when you open them, you aren't in your house anymore! You look around – oh, my...you are ON the rainbow! Wow! You gaze down and can see your house, now just a tiny dot on the ground. You crouch down to touch the rainbow. It feels wet and cool.

Story 7: Rainbow Slide

In fact, you notice the rainbow is quite slippery. Slippery enough to turn into a slide! You take a peek at what lies at the bottom of the rainbow. At the foot of the rainbow lies a big golden pot filled with golden gummy bears! Gummy bears are one of your favorite candies.

You sit down and stretch your legs out in front of you. Using your hands to push forward, you raise your arms over your head as you start to slide "Weeeeeeeee!" you call. You slide down the side of the rainbow, feeling a slight breeze running through your hair. The rainbow feels cool and refreshing underneath your body.

With a little 'plop', you land in the golden pot filled with golden gummy bears. It is soft and bouncy. As you take a deep breath in, you can smell a delicious honey scent. You pick up a gummy bear and bring it up to your nose. 'Sniff, sniff' – it smells like golden honey. You put it in your mouth. Deeeeeelicious!

You flop back into the pile of gummy bears and let out a sigh of happiness. After a few moments of resting on the squishy candy, you climb out of the golden pot and climb back up the side of the rainbow until you are at the top. You continue to slide down the rainbow a few more times, each time being more fun than the last.

As you climb back up to the top of the rainbow one last time, a short little elf is waiting for you. He is wearing a little suit with rainbows all over it, a bright red hat, and elf shoes that curl at the toes. "Hello!" he squeaks. "I'm Sunshine, the Rainbow Elf!" As he extends his hand toward you, you shake it, introducing yourself.

"What do you think of my rainbow?" asks Sunshine. "I love it!" you say. "It makes a fantastic slide, and those gummy bears taste just like honey!".

"Yes, I'm quite proud of my slide," says Sunshine with a big smile. "Have you found out any more secrets about the rainbow yet?" he asks.

Your eyes widen. "No, I only got here a little while ago. What else is there to know?" you ask. Sunshine laughs. "Well it wouldn't be a secret if I told you, would it?!" he says. You ask him for a hint. "Hmm, well you know that saying, 'taste the colors of the rainbow'?" Sunshine asks. You nod your head.

"Well, you can do just that on this rainbow!" says Sunshine, motioning to the ground. You slowly bend down to the floor of the rainbow and carefully look at each color. Your nose starts to tingle with all the aromas curling up into it. You can smell grape, orange, banana, and more. You look up at Sunshine. "Are you meaning to tell me, that I can lick the rainbow?" you ask.

Sunshine chuckles. "Yes!". You lick the red layer – mmm, strawberry shortcake! Next, you lick the orange layer, and it tastes just like a chocolate orange. The yellow is next... banana split, not a big surprise. The green layer of the rainbow tastes like toffee apple; the light blue layer is taffy flavored. Dark blue is blueberry, and violet tastes like sweet grapes! This is the yummiest rainbow you have ever tasted.

"There is one more secret left to learn about this

rainbow!" says Sunshine. "If ever you are feeling stressed or upset about something, simply squeeze your eyes shut and when you open them, you will be back here on this magic rainbow."

You nod your head and tell Sunshine that you will give it a go one day, but for now, you want to keep sliding into the golden pot. You spend the rest of the afternoon sliding up and down and eating honeyflavored gummy bears and licking all the colors of the rainbow.

Your name is being called. You slowly open your eyes and see your mom standing above you, gently waking you. She tells you that you were having a nap but that the rain has cleared up now and you can go outside and play with your friends if you wish. Looking out the window, you see that indeed, the rain has stopped, and peeping out through the sunshine is a beautiful rainbow.

You smile thinking of Sunshine the Rainbow Elf up on his special rainbow in his colorful little suit. Just as you are about to look away, you could almost swear you see someone sliding down the rainbow and landing into a golden pot filled with gummy bears. Laughing, you run outside to meet your friends in the sunshine.

STORY 8
Floating in Space

Getting Comfy

Settle into a cozy and comfortable position. Take a deep breath in, slowly filling up your lungs with air, and then let it all out with a sigh. Feel your body sinking deeper into the bed (*or couch*) and relax your head. If it feels good for you, close your eyes.

Simply listen to the sound of my voice and let your mind drift away.

Think about your little body, lying still and feeling warm. You can feel your chest rising and falling with each breath you take. Think about your feet and ten toes. Maybe your feet are falling out to the side. Maybe they are pointing straight up. However they are positioned is perfect.

Think about your hands and ten fingers. Perhaps your hands are resting next to you or gently resting on your belly. (*Mention mudras only if your child practices them*).

Think about your mouth, your nose, your eyes. Relax them, letting the mouth fall open or stay closed, whichever is comfortable, and let the eyelids grow heavy and fall shut.

You feel completely relaxed, calm, and peaceful. You are safe. You are very loved.

Guided Meditation Story

Today's adventure takes you far, far away, to a place where gravity doesn't exist, where it is always nighttime, and the stars twinkle and shine like bright lights in the sky. A place that houses the eight planets in our solar system. A place where there is no noise, no sounds, just peace and quiet.

Outer space.

You find yourself floating, floating, floating through space. Your body feels weightless and light. Every muscle moves with ease, and you hold no tension. It feels so nice to simply let go of your body and gently drift along.

As you gaze around you, you can see that everything around you is a glowing purple color. The sky is dark blue and is dotted with bright golden stars. Around each star is a purple glow that shines its light out into space. You feel peaceful and safe. It is like everything here moves in slow motion.

In the distance, you can make out the outline of something fluffy, and pale pink, and glittery. As you float closer you see that it is a giant space cloud! It sparkles against the dark blue sky and looks so pretty. The closer you get, the more you can start to smell something sweet.

As you float into the cloud, the smell becomes stronger. Fairy Floss! You stick out your tongue and can taste it in your mouth. It is a giant fairyflossflavored space cloud! As you are enjoying the flavor of candy, you start to notice tiny crackling explosions in your mouth. You look even closer at the cloud and you can see poprock candy sitting within the pink puffiness. You love poprock candy! What a treat.

As you slowly make your way through and out the other end of the pink space cloud, you encounter the next surprise. Up ahead sits a huge, bright orange balloon. What could it be? As you draw closer, it dawns on you. It is a moon rock made out of big, bouncy balloons! It looks just like a bouncy castle.

You land on the moon rock and can immediately feel the squishy surface underneath your feet. It is smooth and soft. You start to bounce up and down. "Weeeeeee!" you call, as you jump higher. You bounce straight up, into space, passing stars and moon clouds on your way. When you get to the top, you slowly float back down again until your feet land on the balloon moon rock with a soft spring.

This moon rock is much more fun than a regular bouncy castle! You continue bouncing, uppppp and downnnnnn, for a while. Outer space is like an amusement park or a funfair, full of rides and candy. You are having such fun. Your body is relaxed as you continue to soar high, up into the dark blue sky.

The next time you jump upwards you look down from your high vantage point and, next to the moon rock made of balloons, you can see something blue and icy. When you land back on the moon rock, you stretch your arms out in front of you and gently float off the rock, making your way toward the ice structure. There is so much to explore in outer space!

The closer you get to the structure, the colder the air becomes. When you arrive, you can see why. It is a small planet made entirely of ice. 'Wow! How cool,' you think. The ice is cool underneath your feet, but not freezing. You like the way it makes a crunching noise each time you take a step.

An iceskating rink in the shape of a star stretches out in front of you. Suddenly, you look down and see a pair of ice skates on the icy floor. You bend down to put them on, tying the shoelaces tight, and wobble over to the entrance of the ice rink. Carefully, you place one foot on the ice, followed by the other.

You take off, gliding over the ice. It feels amazing, spinning, and twirling all over the ice. Everything around you is white, and snowflakes are falling from the sky. It looks like a magical winter wonderland – in outer space!

As you take your final leap, hop, and bound across the ice, you glance over to the side of the rink. A spaceship with polka dots all over it has landed and is waiting for you. You take off your skates and skip over the spaceship. It's time to go home.

You enter the spaceship, taking a seat, and strapping

yourself in. "All aboard!" calls the captain. "The polka dot spaceship is bound for your bedroom!" he calls. You hold on tight as the spaceship chugs up into the air and then, with a smooth *whoosh*, starts to descend back down to earth.

As you are heading down to earth, you hear the captain's voice over the loudspeaker again. "As we journey back home, I would like you to join in a little exercise with me. Close your eyes. Think about planet earth and all the wonderful people that live there. Send them a little bit of your love. Then think about the country you live in and why it is so great. Send it a little bit of your love.

Then, think about your neighborhood and all your friendly neighbors. Send them a little bit of your love. Finally, think about your house and all your beautiful family members. Think about how much you love them and send them a lot of your love."

You find yourself back in bed, warm and cozy, with all your pillows and stuffed animals. What an adventure you have had! You turn your head to look out the window at the night sky, and as you gaze up, you smile, knowing all the magical secrets that space holds.

STORY 9
Zoo Adventure

Getting Comfy

Settle into a cozy and comfortable position. Take a deep breath in, slowly filling up your lungs with air, and then let it all out with a sigh. Feel your body sinking deeper into the bed (*or couch*) and relax your head. If it feels good for you, close your eyes.

Simply listen to the sound of my voice and let your mind drift away.

Think about your little body, lying still and feeling warm. You can feel your chest rising and falling with each breath you take. Think about your feet and ten toes. Maybe your feet are falling out to the side. Maybe they are pointing straight up. However they are positioned is perfect.

Think about your hands and ten fingers. Perhaps your hands are resting next to you or gently resting on your belly. (*Mention mudras only if your child practices them.*)

Think about your mouth, your nose, your eyes. Relax them, letting the mouth fall open or stay closed, whichever is comfortable, and let the eyelids grow heavy and fall shut.

You feel completely relaxed, calm, and peaceful. You are safe. You are very loved.

Guided Meditation Story

As you look out the window at home, the afternoon sun is casting a golden light on the garden. You are really looking forward to this afternoon because you are going to visit a zoo! You can feel the excitement and happiness in your chest and stomach. Life is good.

In the car on the way to the zoo, you think about all the animals you might see. Grizzly lions with soft and fluffy manes. Cheeky monkeys, looking for bananas to eat. Huge, gentle elephants with long trunks. Beautiful giraffes, as tall as a tree. Exotic, stripey zebras, prancing and dancing. You wonder if you will perhaps even find a magic animal. You never know.

You arrive at the zoo. It is buzzing with animal power. All the animals are scattered around in different areas of the zoo. The grass all around is a deep green and there are lots of tall trees and beautiful plants and flowers. As you step out of the car, you can hear the animals singing. "Tweet, tweet," call the birds. "Oink, oink," say the pigs. "Snort, snort," comes from the rhinoceroses. This is going to be a fun evening!

The first stop is the monkey forest. It is a large area with tall trees and vines for the monkeys to climb onto and swing from. A baby monkey with a fuzzy orange head walks up to you for a pat. He nuzzles into your neck. It tickles you. You slowly rub his soft hair, feeling the fur underneath your fingers. He looks up at you, making a cooing noise; he wants a banana!

The zookeeper hands you a bright yellow banana and you peel it for the monkey before handing it to him. He takes it from your hands and stuffs it in his mouth! Cheeky monkey! He looks at you and winks then runs back to his mama, who is watching from afar with a smile. Monkeys are so incredible. *They are so similar to humans*, you think.

Next to the monkey forest is a large enclosure where the lions live. They have watering holes and lots of long grass and ferns to play in. You stand behind a glass wall, watching the lioness of the group. She is lying on a rock, in the late afternoon sun. Her head is tilted in the direction of the sun, but she has her eyes closed.

Suddenly, she opens her eyes and looks directly at you. Your eyes lock with her deep, brown eyes and you both stare at each other for a few moments. Slowly, she stands up and jumps off the rock, walking towards the glass wall. When she is only a few feet away from you, she throws her head back and lets out a mighty roar. "Roooooooooar!"

"Hello, child. I am Lana the Lioness" says the lion, in a low, deep, and gentle voice. "How nice of you to come and visit me and all the animals today," she says. You tell her that this is your first time at the zoo and that you are excited to be here. "We are also excited you are here. We need your help," says Lana.

"I have a note with a message that needs to be delivered to Gerald the Giraffe. Can you please take it and give it to him for me?" asks Lana. "Yes!" you say. "Of course, I will". Lana smiles and fetches a small, folded piece of paper from inside her furry mane. She throws it over the glass wall, and you catch it.

You place the note in your pocket and go off to find the giraffe enclosure. You find it, not too far from the lions. You see three very tall giraffes nibbling at leaves in a tree and one giraffe who is sitting in the corner, crying. Poor thing! "Gerald?" you call out. The crying giraffe stops and sniffs. "Yes. Who are you?" he asks. You tell him who you are and that Lana has sent you.

When he hears Lana's name, his ears prick up and he wanders over to you.

"Why are you crying, Gerald?" you ask.

"I am feeling sad today. One of our favorite zookeepers got a new job at another zoo, and I miss him," explains Gerald. "Well, maybe this will cheer you up," you say, as you hand him the note. Gerald reads the note; his eyes light up and he smiles. He takes in a deep breath as he looks up to the sky.

"Thank you for delivering this to me. I don't need it anymore. I think you should go and find Otto the Otter and tell him Gerald sent you and give him this note, too," he says as he hands the note back to you. He turns around and runs back to the group of giraffes and starts eating leaves.

Story 9: Zoo Adventure

You are curious about what this note says. You open it. It reads: "If you are feeling blue, look up to the sky, take a slow deep breath in, and know that I am thinking of you". *What a nice note*, you think, as you go off in search of Otto the Otter.

After a little while, you find the otters' den. Right away you spot Otto. He is sitting on a rock, with his head in his hands.

"Otto!" you call out. Otto looks up, jumps into the stream of water between you, and swims over. "Yes?" he says.

"You look sad," you say. "I am sad," he replies. "My friends and I built the most beautiful dam in all of the zoo, and during a big storm, it collapsed."

"I'm sorry, Otto. Perhaps this will cheer you up; it's from Gerald the Giraffe," you say as you hand him the note.

Otto opens the note and reads it. He looks up at the sky and smiles to himself. "I feel better after reading this, thank you. It is so nice to have good friends to help you feel better when times are tough," says Otto as he hands you back the note. "You keep it," he says.

You spend the rest of the afternoon wandering around the beautiful zoo, saying hello to all the wonderful animals you see, until the sun sets, and it is evening. It is time to say goodbye, hop back into the car, and head home. When you arrive home, you see a friend of yours sitting on your front doorstep.

They are looking at the ground with a sad look on their face. You race over to them. "Hi! What's wrong?"

you ask them. Your friend tells you that they have had a bad day and wanted to see a friend to cheer them up. You smile and take the note out of your pocket, passing it to them. Your friend opens up the note and reads it, a big smile beginning to form on their face.

"Aww, thanks!" they say and give you a hug. You feel good that you are able to cheer up your friend, because that is what friends are for.

STORY 10
Fruitland

Getting Comfy

Settle into a cozy and comfortable position. Take a deep breath in, slowly filling up your lungs with air, and then let it all out with a sigh. Feel your body sinking deeper into the bed (*or couch*) and relax your head. If it feels good for you, close your eyes.

Simply listen to the sound of my voice and let your mind drift away.

Think about your little body, lying still and feeling warm. You can feel your chest rising and falling with each breath you take. Think about your feet and ten toes. Maybe your feet are falling out to the side. Maybe they are pointing straight up. However they are positioned is perfect.

Think about your hands and ten fingers. Perhaps your hands are resting next to you or gently resting on your belly. (*Mention mudras only if your child practices them*).

Think about your mouth, your nose, your eyes. Relax them, letting the mouth fall open or stay closed, whichever is comfortable, and let the eyelids grow heavy and fall shut.

You feel completely relaxed, calm, and peaceful. You are safe. You are very loved.

Guided Meditation Story

Today, your mom tells you that she is taking you out for a special treat. How lovely! The two of you hop into the car and head towards your destination. After a few minutes, the car pulls up to a delightfullooking fruit store. "We're here!" says your mom. You are so excited, you love fruit!

The entrance to the fruit store looks like a giant piece of watermelon and has big red cherries on either side. You walk inside the store and can smell all different types of fruits. Apple, banana, orange, grape. Your mouth is watering, and you can't wait to sink your teeth into a soft, sweet nectarine.

You gaze around the fruit store. There are tubs of bright green apples, and yellow and orange peaches, little pots of raspberries, blackberries, and boysenberries, trays full of fresh mangoes, and more.

As you wander down into the back of the store, you see a little wooden door at the bottom of a wall. The door has a small handle on it. You are curious as to what is on the other side of the door, so you crouch down, open the door, and crawl through.

What is on the other side of the door makes you

Story 10: Fruitland

gasp. Everything is made out of fruit. You have stepped into a reallife Fruitland! The road is made out of rough coconut shells, the trunks of the trees are bananas, the leaves are slices of mandarin – even the clouds in the sky are soft, fluffy lychees!

What a magical and delicious place! You stoop down to pluck a fruit flower. The petals taste like strawberries. You run over to a forest of trees and take a bite of a tree trunk – mmm, tastes like banana milk! You hear a stream of water running in the distance. You follow the sound of the water and come across a sparkling creek. You realize how thirsty you are.

Cupping your hands together you scoop up the liquid and sip it. Lemonade made from real lemons! A big smile creeps onto your face. You are so happy that you have found a lemonade creek. As you continue drinking, you hear a small voice behind you.

"Welcome to Fruitland!" You spin around and see a cute little strawberry. "Hello! I went through a little door and found myself here," you explain.

"Great! I am happy you are here. I am Sessel the Strawberry!" says the little strawberry. You introduce yourself and tell Sessel how much you love Fruitland.

"Ah, yes. Every little boy or girl that finds themselves in Fruitland falls in love with the place," says Sessel. "If you were feeling sad, gloomy, or unsettled before coming to Fruitland, you will find that you feel much better after you leave!" he says. "Especially if you help me make some calming fruit drops."

As if Sessel can read your mind, he explains that

calming fruit drops are a special type of fruit that relaxes you. "Follow me and we can start cooking," he says as he starts to turn around and scuttle off. You follow him along the rough coconutshell road until it starts to turn into a papayalined path. Up ahead you can see a little fruit house with a melon for a chimney.

You both arrive at the front door, which is made from a giant pineapple. Sessel pushes it open and ushers you inside. "Welcome to my house," he says proudly. You look around at his cottage. Absolutely everything is made from fruit. His table is half of a kiwi fruit and the chairs are made from sweet, chewy raspberries. His couch is a ripe pear, and even his TV is made from fruit!

"Can I pour you a cup of blueberry juice?" asks Sessel. "Yes, please," you reply. Sessel plucks a bunch of blueberries off a blueberry plant on his windowsill in the kitchen and squeezes the berries into a glass. "Here you go," he says, as he places the glass down in front of you. "Fresh blueberry juice!"

You pick up the glass and take a sip of the dark blue juice. It tastes sweet, fruity, and, well, exactly like a blueberry! Delicious.

"Ok, the ingredients we will be using in our calming fruit drops are elderflower, apple, chamomile, and a dash of honey," says Sessel as he collects all the ingredients from various fruitcovered cupboards in the kitchen. "Right," he says, "let's get to work."

Sessel hands you a yellowishwhite elderflower plant and asks you to crush it up with a mortar and pestle.

Story 10: Fruitland

You start to grind the flower, turning it into fine dust. Next, you add in a few chamomile flower petals and grind them into dust too. Once you are done, Sessel collects the ground up flowers and takes them over to a pot on the stove.

He places the flower dust into the pot and adds some choppedup apple and fresh honey, stirring as he goes. Once it starts to bubble, the smell of sweetness from the flowers, apples, and honey begins to fill the room. You take a deep breath in, inhaling the scent.

"We need to let the mixture cool before we place it into molds," says Sessel. While you wait for the mixture to cool down, you spend the afternoon listening to stories from Sessel about his childhood as a baby strawberry and drinking more blueberry juice.

At the end of the afternoon, Sessel hands you a basket full of calming fruit drops. "The chamomile will help relax you, try one," he says; you pop a calming fruit drop into your mouth. It tastes floral, fruity, and sweet, and almost straight away you are filled with a calming sensation throughout your body.

You smile at Sessel and thank him for the gift. "My pleasure!" he squeaks as he leads you to the front door and back along the rough coconutshell road until you arrive back at the little wooden door. You say your farewells before you crawl back through the door to the fruit store.

"Oh, there you are!" says your mom. "Time to head home now! What's in your basket?" she asks.

"Just a little treat to help me feel relaxed," you say,

smiling, thinking of wonderful Fruitland and Sessel the Strawberry.

STORY 11
Talking Teddy Bears

Getting Comfy

Settle into a cozy and comfortable position. Take a deep breath in, slowly filling up your lungs with air, and then let it all out with a sigh. Feel your body sinking deeper into the bed (*or couch*) and relax your head. If it feels good for you, close your eyes.

Simply listen to the sound of my voice and let your mind drift away.

Think about your little body, lying still and feeling warm. You can feel your chest rising and falling with each breath you take. Think about your feet and ten toes. Maybe your feet are falling out to the side. Maybe they are pointing straight up. However they are positioned is perfect.

Think about your hands and ten fingers. Perhaps your hands are resting next to you or gently resting on your belly. (*Mention mudras only if your child practices them*).

Think about your mouth, your nose, your eyes. Relax them, letting the mouth fall open or stay closed, whichever is comfortable, and let the eyelids grow heavy and fall shut.

You feel completely relaxed, calm, and peaceful. You are safe. You are very loved.

Guided Meditation Story

It is a quiet, rainy afternoon and you are in your bedroom playing with your teddy bears. You enjoy being in your bedroom; it is your peaceful, safe place where you know you can always feel relaxed.

You look down at all the teddy bears you have lined up on the floor in front of you. They stare back at you. Their furry little faces look so soft and kind. You bend down to touch their faces. They feel so fluffy beneath your fingers.

Suddenly, one of your teddy bears blinks! You are sure of it. The smallest teddy bear, sitting on the end of the line blinked his little black eyes. You pick him up and hold his face close to yours. Again, he blinks! You set him back down on the floor and take a couple of steps back, still looking at him.

The same teddy bear takes a big yawn and rubs his eyes with his furry little paws. "Don't be afraid! I am Tiny, the friendliest teddy bear you've ever met!" says the teddy bear.

"Actually, you're the only teddy bear I've ever met!" you say.

Story 11: Talking Teddy Bears

Tiny chuckles. "Well, you're about to meet this lot, too" pointing his paw down the line at the rest of your teddy bear collection. Just as he says that all your teddy bears start to wake up, stretching their furry little arms over their heads and yawning. "Wow! Hi, everyone" you say.

One by one, all the teddy bears smile at you and introduce themselves. Even though Tiny is the smallest, he is the leader of the teddy bears. "We watch over you while you sleep at night, protecting you," says Tiny, "and during the day when you are out, we usually sleep, and wake up in the afternoon when you get in."

"What do you do between waking up and watching over me as I sleep?" you ask the group.

"We practice yoga, we meditate, and we chat about all the things we are grateful for!" says your dark brown teddy bear. "How lovely!" you say. "That sounds so relaxing".

"Well, since you're here with us, would you like to join us in our relaxing afternoon activities?" Tiny asks. "I would love to," you reply, as you look out the window at the grey, rainy weather. You look back at the bears and smile. "Well let's get started then!" says Tiny. He gets up and walks into the center of your bedroom.

"Will everyone please gather around for our daily yoga session," he asks the group. One by one, the teddy bears all stand up and hobble over to the space in front of Tiny with their little padded feet. You also stand in front of Teddy, looking around at the others, waiting to see what happens.

"Welcome to today's yoga class. In this class, we will be focusing on moving and stretching our bodies. If you are ever feeling stressed, yoga is a great activity to do as it helps you get out of your own head and focus on something else," says Tiny. The teddy bears all nod in agreement.

Suddenly, lovely music comes floating through the room. You can hear a harp and a violin, a piano, and a gentle trickling of water. The sound of water reminds you of water flowing down a river or creek. The melody is so relaxing you can immediately feel your whole body starting to become looser and relaxed.

Tiny leads you and the other bears through a relaxing yoga flow. You start by sitting down with your legs crossed and taking three deep breaths in and out. In through your nose and out through your nose. After that, Tiny shows you how to stretch your body so you can relax all of your muscles while also making your mind feel calm.

The yoga class finishes with Tiny asking you to all lie down flat on the floor. He explains that this part of the yoga class always happens at the end and is called *Savasana*, or relaxation time. "I would like you to focus on your breathing and let your whole body melt into the floor. Your legs, arms, and head all feel heavy".

As you listen to Tiny's words, you can feel your feet fall to the side; your legs feel like concrete as they sink into the floor, your arms feel relaxed by your side, and your jaw and forehead are at ease. You are holding no tension inside your body whatsoever. It feels really nice. You could lie like this for a long time.

After a few moments, you hear Tiny's voice again. "Slowly and gently, start to bring some movement back into your body. Wriggle your toes and fingers. Raise your arms up over your head and take a nice, big, juicy stretch." You do this and notice how heavenly this stretch feels for you.

Tiny thanks you all for joining his yoga class for the day by pressing his little paws together at his chest and saying "*Namaste*". The rest of the teddy bears answer back "*Namaste*", and all press their paws together at their chests, too. You do the same, smiling at Tiny and the rest of your teddy bears.

"What does '*Namaste*' mean?" you ask Tiny. He says, "*Namaste* means 'I bow to you'. It is a common word used in yoga classes. Teachers and students use this word to say 'thank you' for doing yoga with me."

Tiny ushers you all into a circle and invites you to sit down. "Right, we are going to go around the circle and each says one thing that they are grateful for," says Tiny. Your dark brown teddy bear says he is grateful for having such a beautiful bedroom to live in. Your light brown teddy bear says she is grateful for the daily yoga classes.

It comes around to your turn. You think about all the things you love and everything you have to be grateful for; your mom, your friends, your teachers… "I am grateful that I have learned how to relax today," you say. Tiny smiles and nods his head.

You look out the window, it is starting to get dark. Tiny notices, too, and stands up. "Alright, guys and gals," he claps his hands. "Our afternoon of relaxation has come to an end. We must go back to our positions as our owner will be going to sleep soon and we will need to watch and protect".

The bears all wave goodbye to you. "Bye! It was so nice to meet you all," you call out.

One by one, they march back to their positions on top of your toy box.

Later that night, when you are all tucked up in bed, cozy and warm, you glance over at the teddy bears. Just as you are falling into a deep, comfortable sleep, Tiny winks at you and then goes back dutifully to the job of watching over you for the night.

STORY 12
Art World

Getting Comfy

Settle into a cozy and comfortable position. Take a deep breath in, slowly filling up your lungs with air, and then let it all out with a sigh. Feel your body sinking deeper into the bed (*or couch*) and relax your head. If it feels good for you, close your eyes.

Simply listen to the sound of my voice and let your mind drift away.

Think about your little body, lying still and feeling warm. You can feel your chest rising and falling with each breath you take. Think about your feet and ten toes. Maybe your feet are falling out to the side. Maybe they are pointing straight up. However they are positioned is perfect.

Think about your hands and ten fingers. Perhaps your hands are resting next to you or gently resting on your belly. (*Mention mudras only if your child practices them*).

Think about your mouth, your nose, your eyes. Relax them, letting the mouth fall open or stay closed, whichever is comfortable, and let the eyelids grow heavy and fall shut.

You feel completely relaxed, calm, and peaceful. You are safe. You are very loved.

Guided Meditation Story

Today's adventure takes you to the art gallery. It is the school holidays, and the art gallery is holding a mini art course for children. You are excited to attend; you are going to learn all about drawing, painting, photography, pottery, sculpturing, and more.

You arrive at the art gallery. It is a huge modern building, and, while it looks fairly simple from the outside, you have been told that it houses some of the most amazing art in the world. You enter and take a deep breath; you can actually *smell* the art. It smells new and clean.

On the other side of the foyer, you see a group of children with a teacher. You wander over and see that it is a mini art course. You introduce yourself to the other kids and your teacher. Everyone smiles back at you and the teacher begins to speak to the group.

"Hi, everyone, and welcome to our mini art course!" says the teacher brightly. "Today, we are going to explore different forms of art and various materials that are used to create art. Please stay with the group and don't wander off".

The group assembles into a line and the teacher

Story 12: Art World

leads you through the art gallery. The building is air-conditioned, and it feels nice and cool against your skin.

The first piece of art your teacher shows you all is a big painting of a lake. The lake looks like it is shimmering and the sun in the painting is glowing over it. It looks so real you can almost feel the waves on the water. You close your eyes, and suddenly you can feel the sun shining down on your face.

"How does this painting make you feel?" asks your teacher. Your imagination is interrupted. "It makes me feel peaceful," you say. Your teacher smiles. "That's great. Art can be a very powerful tool to calm the body, and if this painting makes you feel peaceful then I think you have a good eye for art," she says.

Your teacher leads you and the other kids on to the next piece of art. It is a black and white drawing of a little girl. She has long, curly hair and seems to be looking right at you. You gasp. The drawing is so lifelike, and you can see a glimmer of fun and mischief in her eyes. You stare at her as the teacher talks about the drawing, explaining the technique the artist used.

It is time to head off to a new piece of art, but just as you turn to follow the group, the girl in the drawing waves at you. "No way!" you think. You move closer to the drawing. "Psssst!" whispers the girl in the drawing. "This way."

She uses her hand to usher you into the painting. You stare at her in amazement as you feel the ground come away from under you. Oomph! You land with a thud, flat on your bottom.

When you look up, you cannot believe your eyes. The girl in the drawing is standing in front of you with her hands clasped together in delight. "I thought you would never come in!" she says in delight. "Welcome to Art World!"

You look around you. Everything is brightly colored. The grass is painted a light green and the trees have been sketched. There is a stream of water in the distance which looks like it has been created out of different blue crayons. The sun in the sky is a bright yellow and has been painted with watercolors. Your wide eyes must have said it all.

The girl laughs. "It's okay! Art World is a lot of fun. I'm Lottie," she says as she sticks out her hand. You shake it and introduce yourself. "Only those who have a good eye for art are allowed into Art World, so congratulations on being chosen!" beams Lottie. You smile; Art World is definitely beautiful!

"Come on, let me show you around," says Lottie, grabbing your hand and leading you towards the town of Art World. All the buildings are covered in large, colorful spots of paint – even the pavement is painted with different pictures and doodles. Lottie leads you to a white building. It is the only building that isn't covered in color.

"This building has been waiting for you to cover it in your art," says Lottie. You look up at the big building, or rather, blank canvas. "Oh, my," you say.

Story 12: Art World

Lottie rolls a cart over to you. On the cart are all sorts of different paints, crayons, pastels, chalk, markers, paintbrushes, and more. "Go wild!" says Lottie.

You pick up a thick paintbrush and dip it into the blue paint. The paint coats the bristles of the paintbrush and you hold it up to the wall of the building, creating your first blue line. The paint easily rolls onto the wall. Once you start, you can't seem to stop. You paint shapes, long and short lines, swirls, flowers. You use green, red, yellow, and purple paint.

Next, you pick up a little balloon filled with silver paint and throw it at the wall. The balloon explodes like a water bomb and the silver paint splatters the wall. It looks great and it feels so good to just hurl the balloon at the wall. You pick up another paintfilled balloon. This one has gold paint in it. The gold paint explodes all over the wall, mixing in with the silver.

You see little pots of multicolored glitter and pick one of them up. You pinch some glitter in between your thumb and fingers and sprinkle it all over the wall. This wall is starting to look so pretty and colorful. You are giggling with happiness and Lottie is enjoying watching you.

Each time you add to the wall, you notice your body feeling lighter. Any stress you have is melting away. Your head, neck, and shoulders feel so loose. Your breathing is easy and calm. You pick up a bright yellow piece of chalk and draw a heart on the wall. It feels magnificent.

Lottie and you spend the rest of the afternoon

covering the building in art. The two of you lose yourself in the paints, brushes, glitter, and chalk. You look over at Lottie. She has orange paint smeared all over her face. You laugh. She looks at you and also laughs. There is purple and green paint all over your nose, through your hair, and all over your hands.

You are having so much fun, that you almost forget about your teacher and the rest of the group on the art course. "Lottie! I have had such a fun time today, but I really should be getting back to the art gallery," you say. Lottie tells you she understands and leads you by the hand back to where you whooshed in from the gallery. She hugs you tightly.

"It was lovely to meet you. You are very talented, and just remember, any time you are feeling tense and stressed, know that art is always there for you. It is a great way to release stress." says Lottie. You nod and thank her, hugging her back.

You close your eyes and squeeze them hard. When you open them, you are back in the art gallery, looking back at the painting of Lottie. She waves at you as you whisper your goodbyes and run off to find the rest of the group.

At the end of the day, on your way back home, your mom asks you what you learned about today. You tell her that you had the opportunity to decorate and create art on the wall of a large building. Your mom looks at you in the rearview mirror and smiles. "That is wonderful," she says.

"Yep! And I learned that being creative is a great

way to help me feel calm. I noticed creating art really focused my mind," you say.

"Well, then!" says your mom. "We will have to send you back to the art gallery more often."

You nod your head in agreement; you would love that.

YOUR FREE BONUS
The Beginners Guide to Mudras for Kids!

As a way of thanking you for your purchase, I have a **free bonus** to offer you.

Besides the beautiful meditation and bedtime stories provided in this book, I have created **The Beginners Guide to Mudras for Kids,** which will teach your kids the hand symbols they can use during a guided meditation story. The guide explains why mudras are beneficial and what it all means. Your kids will master the main mudras in no time.

Click (or tap) below to get your FREE Bonus instantly.

Click here:
https://www.mangobroom.com/mudras-kids/

STORY 13
The Friendly Pirates

Getting Comfy

Settle into a cozy and comfortable position. Take a deep breath in, slowly filling up your lungs with air, and then let it all out with a sigh. Feel your body sinking deeper into the bed (*or couch*) and relax your head. If it feels good for you, close your eyes.

Simply listen to the sound of my voice and let your mind drift away.

Think about your little body, lying still and feeling warm. You can feel your chest rising and falling with each breath you take. Think about your feet and ten toes. Maybe your feet are falling out to the side. Maybe they are pointing straight up. However they are positioned is perfect.

Think about your hands and ten fingers. Perhaps your hands are resting next to you or gently resting on your belly. (*Mention mudras only if your child practices them*).

Think about your mouth, your nose, your eyes. Relax them, letting the mouth fall open or stay closed, whichever is comfortable, and let the eyelids grow heavy and fall shut.

You feel completely relaxed, calm, and peaceful. You are safe. You are very loved.

Guided Meditation Story

It is a beautiful sunny day. The sky is blue and clear, and the weather is perfect. You are with your family out on a boat, sailing the seven seas. Well, not quite, but you are on a lovely little yacht in the ocean. You've been swimming in the deep, blue ocean and you even went snorkeling and saw all the amazing different fish and coral.

You can feel the wind in your hair, and you can smell the salt from the ocean. The boat is shiny, white, and smooth. Everyone is having a good time. You can feel the ocean bump, bump, bumping underneath the boat. They are tiny bumps because the waves are gentle. Sitting on a comfy big chair on the deck, you feel relaxed. The rhythm of the boat makes you feel sleepy and you can feel yourself start to nod off.

The chair feels so soft and as the sunlight shines down on your body, you drift off into a lovely little nap. The sounds of the ocean and your family begin to fade, and you find yourself in that dreamy stage between being awake and being asleep.

When you open your eyes, you aren't on the yacht anymore. You lift your head and glance around you.

Story 13: The Friendly Pirates

You are still on the ocean, but you are now in a much bigger boat – a ship, in fact. The ship is made from wood, and when you look up you see a black flag flying from the very top of the mast. The flag has a skull and crossbones on it, but the skull is smiling and on top of the flag it says, "The Friendly Pirates."

Where am I? you wonder. Suddenly, you hear a loud "screeeeeeeeetch" and you see a red, green, and yellow parrot flapping its feathers, flying towards you. The parrot lands on your shoulder. "Hello, hello, hello!" squawks the parrot. "I'm Pippy the Parrot! Pippy the Parrot! Pippy the Parrot!"

"Hi, Pippy! Where on earth am I?" you ask. "Welcome to the Friendly Pirates ship! Friendly Pirates!" screeches Pippy.

"Where is everyone?" you ask Pippy. "On their way! On their way!" says Pippy.

In the distance, you can hear laughter. You look over the railings of the ship and see a small dinghy rowing towards the ship. You can make out five people in the dinghy and they are all laughing and smiling. As they row closer, they spot you. "Arrr! Finally, you've come! We've been waitin' for ya!" says one of the pirates.

They arrive at the ship and climb up the sides on rope ladders, lugging a big chest with them. They dump the chest on the deck.

The tallest pirate steps forward. He wipes his wet hand on his pants and then stretches it out. "Nice to meet ya! I am Fred, the Captain of the Friendly Pirates!"

he says. "Next to me is my wife, Frederika, and these are our three sons: Filip, Frank, and Ferdinand."

Frederika gives you a warm smile. Their sons all say hello and tell you they could use a fourth friendly pirate. "But I'm not a pirate," you say. "I don't even know what pirates do."

"Arrr. Well, most pirates sail the seven seas and pillage other ships. But we are the Friendly Pirates, and we don't do that. We help others," says Fred.

"Help others?" you ask. "Yes!" says Frederika. "We sail the seas looking for those who are in need of help. Actually, we are going back out in the dinghy in a few minutes to help a whale find her baby. Would you like to come?"

You tell them you would love to go. You and the Friendly Pirates pile into the little dinghy and off you go. The boys are using paddles to move the boat along. As you move through the water, Frederika starts to make a loud, highpitched call. "Ohhhhhhhhh, Oooowoohhhhhhh" she calls. After a few moments, a huge whale appears before the dinghy.

The whale is beautiful. She is huge, with grey skin and amazing dark eyes. Something about her eyes looks so sad, though. "Have you found her?" the whale asks.

"Not yet, but we are still looking," says Fred. "Please find my baby. I am so worried" says the whale before she dips back under the ocean and swims off.

With a determined look in their eyes, the Friendly Pirates set off, Frederika calling out for the baby every few minutes. "Ohhhhhhhwooooohhhhh!".

"Where did you learn how to do a whale call?" you ask her. She smiles. "We are the Friendly Pirates, we can communicate with all the animals that live in the ocean," she says.

As you continue paddling, you notice a big rock up ahead. As you get closer, you can see something large and grey on the rock. "Look!" you point towards the rock. The Friendly Pirates turn and look at the rock. "Oh, my! It looks like the baby whale is beached on that rock" says Frederika.

The boys quickly paddle the dinghy over to the rock. "Help me!" squeals the baby whale. "I am stuck and cannot move!"

The boys throw an anchor down into the ocean, so the dinghy stops and is still. You all climb out of the dinghy and onto the rock. "Quick!" says Frederika. "You and I will splash her with water to keep her skin moist and hydrated, and the boys can push her off this rock."

You cup your hands together and dip them into the ocean, filling your hands with water. You throw the water onto the baby whale's skin. Her skin is so soft and smooth. "Ahh, thank you!" calls the baby whale. "I needed that water". You continue to fill your hands with water, cooling the baby whale down.

Meanwhile, Fred and the boys push the baby whale into the direction of the ocean. They grunt as they push. Even a baby whale is very heavy! "And push again!" calls Fred. The boys give one final push, and the baby whale slides off the rock, back into the ocean.

"Thank you!" she calls, as she twirls and flips, clapping her fins together. "You have saved me!" The Friendly Pirates all cheer and thank you for helping. "If you hadn't spotted the baby whale on the rock, we may not have found her," says Fred. You smile. You feel good. It is nice to have helped others.

"Wait here," Frederika tells the baby whale. "Let me call your mother". Frederika lets out a whale call: "Ohhhhhhwoohhhhhh…ohhhhhhohhhhhh…ohhhhhhwoohhhhhh." A few moments later the mother whale appears underneath the surface of the water. She sticks her head out of the ocean and when she sees her baby swimming excitedly towards her, she lets out a long whale call of happiness.

The mother and baby embrace one another. "Thank you, thank you, thank you!" the mother whale calls out to you and the Friendly Pirates. "I cannot thank you enough for helping to find and saving my baby. I would like to repay you by giving you all this treasure chest I found at the bottom of the ocean floor."

The mother whale tosses a brown, rusty chest into the dinghy with her fins. You all thank her as you watch her and her baby swim away into the sunset. "Right!" says Fred. "Let's get back to the ship so we can break open this chest and see what's inside!"

The boys paddle the dinghy back to the ship, where you all climb back onto the ship, bringing the chest aboard with you. You look at the locked chest and wonder what could be inside. Maybe the chest holds hundreds of gold coins. Or perhaps it holds dozens of jewels and diamonds. Maybe it even holds a secret map that leads to more treasure!

Fred grabs a hammer and breaks the lock on the chest. Very slowly, he opens the chest. You peer inside. Sitting at the very bottom of the chest is a red heart the size of your hand. Fred picks up the heart and takes it out of the chest.

"Arrr," he says. "The heart of the ocean." He gently cups the heart in his hands and closes his eyes, taking in a deep breath. When he opens his eyes, you notice how bright and sparkly his eyes are. He smiles and passes the heart to his son, Filip. Filip also cups the heart in his hands, closing his eyes and taking in a deep breath.

When all the Friendly Pirates have held the heart, it is your turn. Frederika passes you the heart. You take it in your hands. Immediately, you feel warmth in your hands. You close your eyes and feel the warm glow spreading around your entire body.

It spreads from your hands up your arms, across your shoulders, to your chest, down to your belly, moving its way down to your thighs, your knees, your calves, your ankles, and down into your feet, spreading to each one of your toes. The glow then zips back up to your throat, spreading to your chin, your cheeks, your nose, eyes, forehead, and warms up your whole head.

When you open your eyes, you feel something inside of you that you haven't felt so intensely before. It is a powerful feeling. You feel so happy, content, and simply full of love. You look around at the Friendly Pirates who are looking back at you, smiling warmly.

"The heart of the ocean is special," says Frederika. "It is delivered to us each time we help someone or do a good deed. It teaches us about unconditional love – love that knows no limits. The heart of the ocean and all that it makes us feel is our reward," she says.

You smile at the Friendly Pirates.

In the distance, you can hear your name being called. Gently, you open your eyes. You are back on the deck chair on the yacht. You fell asleep! You look around you. The sun is starting to set over the ocean and the sky is beginning to turn a purplepink color. Your family tells you that the day on the ocean has come to an end and it is time to go home.

As you slowly climb off the yacht and place your feet onto the wooden dock, you turn around to look back at the ocean one last time. Far away, in the distance, you can just make out a faint outline of a big ship. On the ship are five figures, one of them with a parrot sitting on his shoulder, waving goodbye at you as a mother whale and her baby bob in the water in front of them.

STORY 14
The Grand Dance of the Seahorses

Getting Comfy

Settle into a cozy and comfortable position. Take a deep breath in, slowly filling up your lungs with air, and then let it all out with a sigh. Feel your body sinking deeper into the bed (or *couch*) and relax your head. If it feels good for you, close your eyes.

Simply listen to the sound of my voice and let your mind drift away.

Think about your little body, lying still and feeling warm. You can feel your chest rising and falling with each breath you take. Think about your feet and ten toes. Maybe your feet are falling out to the side. Maybe they are pointing straight up. However they are positioned is perfect.

Think about your hands and ten fingers. Perhaps your hands are resting next to you or gently resting on

your belly. (*Mention mudras only if your child practices them*).

Think about your mouth, your nose, your eyes. Relax them, letting the mouth fall open or stay closed, whichever is comfortable, and let the eyelids grow heavy and fall shut.

You feel completely relaxed, calm, and peaceful. You are safe. You are very loved.

Guided Meditation Story

Today, you are on vacation with your family. School's out for the summer and there are fun and relaxing vibes in the air. Your family has taken a trip to a beachside town. The sun is shining, it is a hot day, the sky is bright blue, and you are spending the day at the beach.

As soon as you arrive at the beach, you put on your snorkel and flippers and make your way down to the water's edge. You wade in a little way and find the temperature of the water is pleasant. You make your way into waistdeep water before stretching your arms out in front of you and kicking off, your flippers propelling you ahead.

You feel the water rushing past your body, making tiny air bubbles around your hands and feet. You love this feeling of freedom. The ocean is yours and you can spin, twirl, and move as fast or as slow as you want. A school of brightly colored fish swims past you. You wonder where they are going. Do they have a house under the ocean, or do they live amongst the green sea plants?

You dip your face into the water, eyes wide open behind your divemask. The water is clear, and you can see the amazing and magical underwater world – delicate coral, brightly colored starfish lazing around on rocks, the soft sand at the bottom of the seafloor. It all looks so beautiful.

Out of the corner of your eye, you see something swim past you. You spin around to take a better look. Bobbing, in front of your eyes is the loveliest seahorse you have ever seen. It is tiny, about the size of the palm of your hand. The seahorse's body is orange, dotted with yellow splotches, and it has little black eyes with long curly eyelashes.

"Hi!" squeaks the seahorse. You wave back at the seahorse. She swims towards your face and comes up close to your eyes. Slowly, she flutters her long eyelashes against yours. After a few moments, she swims back. "That is a seahorse's way of saying 'nice to meet you!'" she says. You open your mouth to speak and amazingly, you can. "Nice to meet you too!" You are surprised to realize you can speak underwater.

"I have put a spell on you!" squeaks the seahorse. "When you are with me, you can talk and breathe underwater!" You breathe in through your nose and out through your mouth. It works perfectly. "That is so cool!" you tell the seahorse.

"Oh, I am sorry – I am so rude, I forgot to introduce myself," says the seahorse. "I am Cornelia the seahorse and we have been waiting for you." You ask Cornelia who she is talking about. "Myself and the other seahorses. We are in the middle of creating a seahorse dance, but we are finding some of the dance moves a little bit tricky. Would you come with me and help us create our seahorse dance?" Cornelia asks.

You nod; you would love to help out! You have never hung out with a group of seahorses before. Cornelia tells you to paddle your feet hard and follow her. She dips down, deep into the depths of the ocean, and you follow her. Her little seahorse tail moves elegantly and quickly through the water.

After a few minutes, she stops on the bottom of the ocean floor. You are able to stand on the sandy, ocean floor and look around. The most beautiful sea creatures are floating around you.

"Welcome to the bottom of the ocean," squeaks Cornelia. "It is so beautiful, quiet, and peaceful," you tell her. "Yep!" she replies, "And everyone around here is super friendly."

A multicolored giant manta ray swims up to you and gently floats around your face, caressing your forehead with the tip of his wing. "This is Mervin the Manta!" Cornelia says. "He is the loveliest manta ray in the whole ocean, and he loves new guests." You smile at Mervin and pat his skin. It feels so soft underneath your fingers.

Swimming together in a little group, about ten seahorses emerge from behind Cornelia. Aha! These must be the dancing seahorses she was talking about.

Story 14: The Grand Dance of the Seahorses

They come forward one by one and introduce themselves. They are excited you are there, and all are keen to start dancing. "Ok, so we will show you what we have so far, and then we will ask for your thoughts," says Cornelia.

The seahorses all step back and form a straight line. "Hit it, Mervin!" calls Cornelia. Mervin the Manta clicks "Play" on a little device and the sound of music lights up the ocean. It sounds like there are speakers everywhere and the bottom of the ocean floor is transformed into a giant concert hall. You can hear violins, cellos, harps, flutes, and the piano.

The seahorses glide and twirl, somersault and prance. Their dance is amazing, but you do notice that they are not in sync and sometimes they are not in beat to the glorious music. After a few moments, the seahorses end their dance by all doing headstands in a row, except for the smallest seahorse. She tries to do a headstand, but she keeps tumbling forward and can't keep her balance.

"So," says Cornelia, "what do you think?"

"I think it is a lovely dance and the music is brilliant," you respond, "but there are a few things I think I can help you guys out with." The seahorses all gather around you, bobbing up and down in excitement. This time, it is your turn to say: "Hit it, Mervin!" The music comes on.

You line up all the seahorses and direct them all to twirl at the same time, using your hands to point and direct them. You feel like a music composer! When it comes up to the part where they somersault, you point at Cornelia and she somersaults into the middle of the group and as you point to each seahorse, one by one, they all gracefully somersault into the middle too. It looks perfect!

Towards the end of the dance, you move closer to the smallest seahorse. As the rest of the seahorses move into a headstand, you stand next to the smallest seahorse and help support her by keeping one hand on her tail and one hand on her body as she stands on her head. She balances and stays in her headstand for as long as the others.

When they are finished, the seahorses all thank you. "Wow! We have been practicing for a long time, but this is the first time we completed the dance smoothly and without any mistakes," says Cornelia. You tell the seahorses that you were happy to help.

The smallest seahorse comes over to you. "We, the seahorses, hereby invite you to the 'Grand Dance of the Seahorses' next month," she says. You tell them that you would be delighted and that you better be getting back to shore, but you will be back next month to watch their live concert. They wish you farewell, and Cornelia leads you back to the beach.

You swim ashore and head back up to your family. The sand is still warm, but the sun is starting to set, and it is time for you to head home.

Later that evening as you lay in bed, you close your eyes and can hear the magnificent music and see the dance of the seahorses. You smile. You cannot wait to join them again soon.

STORY 15
The Dog Park

Getting Comfy

Settle into a cozy and comfortable position. Take a deep breath in, slowly filling up your lungs with air, and then let it all out with a sigh. Feel your body sinking deeper into the bed (*or couch*) and relax your head. If it feels good for you, close your eyes.

Simply listen to the sound of my voice and let your mind drift away.

Think about your little body, lying still and feeling warm. You can feel your chest rising and falling with each breath you take. Think about your feet and ten toes. Maybe your feet are falling out to the side. Maybe they are pointing straight up. However they are positioned is perfect.

Think about your hands and ten fingers. Perhaps your hands are resting next to you or gently resting on your belly. (*Mention mudras only if your child practices them*).

Think about your mouth, your nose, your eyes. Relax them, letting the mouth fall open or stay closed, whichever is comfortable, and let the eyelids grow heavy and fall shut.

You feel completely relaxed, calm, and peaceful. You are safe. You are very loved.

Guided Meditation Story

You are on a little walk around your neighborhood. It is a nice, warm afternoon. Other children are outside, playing on the footpaths; people are watering their gardens, and spring is in the air. Up ahead, you can see a big, green, grassy park with tall trees, park benches, and a lot of shade.

You wander toward the park and find a bench to sit on, underneath the branches of a big oak tree. Your feet don't quite reach the ground, so you swing your legs back and forth, enjoying the feeling. You close your eyes and take a deep breath in through your nose and slowly release the air out of your nose. Sometimes, it is just nice to sit still and enjoy your surroundings.

As you open your eyes, you feel something at your feet. You look down; a small puppy is playing with your shoelaces. You giggle, watching the puppy chewing and pulling on your shoelaces. Climbing off the bench, you squat down so you can pat the puppy. His hair is silky and soft, and he has bright blue eyes. His little tail wags quickly as he looks up at you with those puppydog eyes.

"Incomingggggg!" – a small brown chihuahua

comes flying over and runs headfirst into the puppy. "Ow!" cries the puppy as he tumbles backward onto his bottom. You stand up, your eyes wide. "You guys can talk?" you ask the two dogs. "Of course, we can talk! We're dogs!" says the chihuahua.

"Welcome to the dog park," says the puppy in a soft voice. "I'm Tommy, and this is my silly friend, Pico," he says, pointing his paw toward the chihuahua. "Nice to meet you!" says Pico, giving you a big grin. "Hi, nice to meet you both. I have never met talking dogs before," you say. Pico looks at you and laughs. "That's a funny joke," he says.

Tommy comes towards you and gently tugs on the bottom of your pants. "Come with us, we'll introduce you to the rest of the group." The two dogs lead, and you follow.

Up ahead are two fluffy poodles; one is black, and one is white. They are standing next to each other, watching the rest of the dogs playing. "Hi, ladies, this is our new friend," says Tommy as he introduces you to the poodles.

The poodles look down their snouts at you. "Charmed, I'm sure," says the black poodle. "How do you do?" asks the white poodle. "Don't worry about them!" says Pico. "They're known to be a couple of snobs," he says, laughing. You smile at the poodles. "I'm good, thank you, how are you?" you ask them.

"Quite well, thank you," says the white poodle. "We are patiently waiting for the Ecstatic Dance class to start," says the black poodle. "The *what* dance class?" you ask. The Poodles sigh impatiently.

"Ecstatic Dance is a lot of fun!" says Pico. "It is a type of dance where you simply listen to the beat and rhythm of the music and move your body in any way you want," he says. "It's a great way to release stress and let your body move," adds Tommy. You tell the dogs that you've never heard of this type of dancing before, but you are excited to try it out.

All of a sudden, you notice the dogs all stop playing and barking and look toward one large blackandwhite-spotted dalmatian walking into the center of the park. She is carrying a large speaker and a smartphone in her mouth. She turns to face all of the dogs.

"Welcome, furry friends, to our Ecstatic Dance class," she says. All the dogs in the park start cheering. The Dalmatian spots you. "Why, hello, twolegged friend! Welcome. Are you here to dance with us?" she asks you. "Yes, I would love to dance with you," you say. The Dalmatian smiles at you.

"Remember, let the music move your body and let go of all your worries! We are here to relax and enjoy," the dalmatian tells you and all the dogs. They all nod, as do you. The dalmatian picks up her smartphone and connects it to the speakers. "Let's dance!" she calls out as she presses *Play*.

Strong tribal music starts to float out of the speakers. It has a deep beat, and you can feel the bass in your body. You look around you. Pico is wriggling his whole body, including his tail. His eyes are closed, and he is completely lost in the music. Tommy is swaying from sidetoside, grinning at you. The two poodles are dancing the salsa!

You can feel the music take hold of your body and you feel your feet start to move. Before you know it, you let go of any shyness you had and start to move, jump, twist and shake. It feels so good to release all the energy from your body and simply dance. The next song comes on and it makes you want to shimmy your hips and clap your hands. You are having a great time!

There are dogs doing cartwheels, dogs dancing on their back legs, dogs dancing like ballerinas; it is amazing to see! The large dalmatian is dancing by herself. She is stomping her paws into the ground and howling up at the sky. Every so often, she turns around in a circle and kicks up her paws.

Tommy and Pico dance over toward you and take your hands in their paws. The three of you form a little circle, making the circle smaller and yelling "Opa!" and then dancing back out to make the circle wider.

"I have an idea! Let's start a conga line!" says Pico. He holds onto Tommy's waist and you hold onto Pico's waist as you dance around in a line. One by one the other dogs dance over to you and join the conga line. 'One, two, chachacha!' you all cry as the line grows longer. The dalmatian is at the end of the line, throwing back her head and howling.

You spend the rest of the afternoon dancing like this until you notice the sun is beginning to set. You turn to your furry friends. "This has been so much fun!" you say. "But all this dancing has made me really tired and I must be getting home." The dogs all dance over to you and give you big hugs. You wave goodbye at the dalmatian and she winks back at you.

You leave the park, taking one last glance over your shoulder at all the dancing dogs, dancing to the beat and rhythm of the music, howling up at the sky as the moon starts to emerge. When you get home, you collapse into your bed. All the dancing has made you very tired!

You put on your pajamas and crawl into bed, snuggling down into your blanket. Visions of dancing dogs float through your head. You look out of your bedroom window and up at the moon, saluting it with a silent howl. Resting your head into the pillow, you nod off into a deep sleep, dreaming of poodles doing the salsa.

STORY 16
Snow Globe

Getting Comfy

Settle into a cozy and comfortable position. Take a deep breath in, slowly filling up your lungs with air, and then let it all out with a sigh. Feel your body sinking deeper into the bed (*or couch*) and relax your head. If it feels good for you, close your eyes.

Simply listen to the sound of my voice and let your mind drift away.

Think about your little body, lying still and feeling warm. You can feel your chest rising and falling with each breath you take. Think about your feet and ten toes. Maybe your feet are falling out to the side. Maybe they are pointing straight up. However they are positioned is perfect.

Think about your hands and ten fingers. Perhaps your hands are resting next to you or gently resting on your belly. (*Mention mudras only if your child practices them*).

Think about your mouth, your nose, your eyes. Relax them, letting the mouth fall open or stay closed, whichever is comfortable, and let the eyelids grow heavy and fall shut.

You feel completely relaxed, calm, and peaceful. You are safe. You are very loved.

Guided Meditation Story

You are all snuggled up by the fireplace, watching the snowfall through the window outside. You feel cozy and warm in your pajamas as you watch the snowflakes float through the air and softly land on the ground. Everything outside is coated in a white blanket of powder. The grass, the birdbath, the shed, your bike – are all covered in snow.

You turn your gaze to the fireplace. Behind the fireguard, the flames are bright orange and red. You stretch your arm out in front of you like a cat to warm your hands by the fire. After a few moments, you raise your hands to your face and touch your cheeks. Your face is already warm, but your hands warm your skin even more.

You turn to look back out of the window and notice a snow globe sitting on the windowsill. You pick it up to inspect it further. Inside the glass ball is a little snowman with blue mittens, a scarf, and a beanie on his head. He has a carrot for a nose and two little raisin eyes. He is standing next to a little log cottage and there are lots of pine trees scattered around. You shake the snow globe.

Story 16: Snow Globe

Hundreds of little white flakes fly around the globe and it looks like it is also snowing where the snowman lives. You put down the snow globe and curl up in your chair. You are feeling tired and your eyelids feel heavy. As you drift off into sleep, you think about all the fun the snowman must have living in a magical winterworld.

You wake to see small flames dancing in between the logs in the fireplace; you sit up, looking out the window. Standing there is a snowman! He is wearing blue mittens, a scarf, and a beanie! He has a carrot for a nose and raisins as eyes. *That looks exactly like the snowman from the snow globe*, you think.

You quickly put on your snow boots, a big, fleecy, warm jacket, mittens, a scarf, and a beanie and open the front door. Your feet make a crunching noise in the snow as you walk toward the snowman. The air is fresh on your face. You can feel it dancing on your cheeks, nose, chin, lips, and forehead.

Standing in front of the snowman, you notice he also has a big smile, made out of little twigs. You smile back at him, wondering how he got there.

"Hello! You found me!" says the snowman.

"I think you found me!" you say back. "I fell asleep and when I woke up, you were standing in my front garden."

"I hope you're warm in those clothes, because we are about to go on a ride," says the snowman. "I'm Percy, by the way, nice to meet you!"

You tell Percy you are super warm and that your

jacket is made for the snow. "Where are we going, Percy?" you ask.

"You'll see!" says Percy, with a big smile. He whistles loudly and, out of nowhere, a big, bright, white vehicle pulls up in front of the two of you. The vehicle is shiny and has four wheels.

"This is the Snow Mobile! I use it to get around everywhere. It's really fun to ride on. Want to come for a drive?" asks Percy.

"Sure!" you say. You and Percy both climb into the snowmobile and adjust your seatbelts, pulling the straps across your bodies nice and tight.

"To my house!" says Percy. The snowmobile starts up and before you know it, you're whipping down the street. You can feel the cold air against your face as you squint your eyes shut so snowflakes don't fall in them.

After a few moments, you arrive at Percy's house. It is a cute little log cottage with green pine trees all around. This scene looks familiar! You and Percy climb out of the snowmobile and Percy leads you into his home.

As soon as you walk inside, the hot air warms your face. It is so toasty. Percy's fireplace is crackling, and you can hear the sound of a kettle whistling.

"Just in time, the tea is ready!" says Percy as he walks over to the kettle to prepare the tea. You take off your snow boots, your jacket, mittens, scarf, and beanie and hang them up. You look around you. Percy's house is delightful. In front of the fireplace is a brown furry rug

Story 16: Snow Globe

with two soft-looking armchairs. He has shelves full of books and even a Christmas tree in the corner!

"Percy, why do you have a Christmas tree in the middle of February!?" you ask.

"Because in my world, it is always Christmas! Every day!" he says as he invites you to sit in one of the big comfy armchairs. You sit down before he hands you a big mug of steaming tea. You smell it, taking a deep, deep breath in through your nose and an even bigger breath out through your mouth. It smells like cinnamon and mandarin.

Percy sits down in the other chair with his mug of tea. He takes a sip and smiles at you.

"Percy, I have a question," you say. "You are made of ice. So, don't you get too hot and melt when you're inside, especially in front of a fireplace?" you ask.

Percy chuckles. "Yes, I am made of ice, but it is a magic kind of ice. I don't melt when I am inside – I don't feel the heat and I don't feel the cold," he says.

You think about this as you sip on your tea, glancing over at all the books on the shelves. Percy notices you looking at them.

"Would you like me to read to you?" asks Percy.

"That would be lovely," you say.

Percy gets up and walks over to the shelf. He runs his hand along a row of colored books. Some books are thin, others are thick. He chooses a dark green book and brings it back to his chair. He opens the first page and reads the title: "Relaxation for Children."

"Settle down into a comfy position in your chair," Percy tells you. "Close your eyes and find stillness."

You relax into the armchair and close your eyes. Your body feels heavy as he continues to read with a slow, calm voice.

"Take a deep breath in through your nose and out through your nose. And another, breathing in deeply, filling up your lungs, and let it all out back through your nose. Imagine a glow, starting at your feet. This glow laces around your toes, warming them up and filling you with positive energy.

"Now, imagine this glow moving up to your ankles and onto your knees and the backs of them. You can feel its warmth. Slowly, it creeps up to your thighs and into your belly. It feels so nice, this glow, as it sits in your belly for a few moments. It moves on up to your chest and spreads out to your shoulders, gliding down your arms and into your hands.

You can feel the warmth in each finger – your pinky fingers all the way to your thumbs. The glow spreads back up your arms and shoulders and into your throat. It feels like you have swallowed honey. It is warm and smooth in your throat. The glow moves up to your chin, your mouth, your cheeks, your nose, your eyes, and your forehead, where it stays for a few moments.

You can feel your face warming up, almost as if the sun is gently beaming down on it. The glow then creeps up to the crown of your head, the very top of your scalp, and covers your whole body. You sit like this for

Story 16: Snow Globe

a few moments, basking in this glow. It makes you feel happy, calm, relaxed, and positive," reads Percy.

Listening to Percy's words has made you feel super floppy, relaxed, and calm. Your breathing is soft, and you feel so happy and at ease. You open your eyes and sleepily smile at Percy.

"Thanks, Percy, that was lovely. I feel so relaxed," you say.

"You're welcome," says Percy. He looks out the window. "It's getting dark, we'd best get you back home," he says as he gets up. You put your warm clothes back on and you both head outside toward the Snowmobile.

Percy whisks you through the evening air back to your house.

"Thank you so much, Percy, I had a wonderful and relaxing time listening to your guided relaxation for children," you say.

"My pleasure," smiles Percy. "Now go inside, before you catch a cold out here!"

You run toward your front door and turn around to wave Percy goodbye. He honks the horn and takes off in the Snowmobile, whizzing back down the street into the wintery night.

STORY 17
The Magic Sandpit

Getting Comfy

Settle into a cozy and comfortable position. Take a deep breath in, slowly filling up your lungs with air, and then let it all out with a sigh. Feel your body sinking deeper into the bed (*or couch*) and relax your head. If it feels good for you, close your eyes.

Simply listen to the sound of my voice and let your mind drift away.

Think about your little body, lying still and feeling warm. You can feel your chest rising and falling with each breath you take. Think about your feet and ten toes. Maybe your feet are falling out to the side. Maybe they are pointing straight up. However they are positioned is perfect.

Think about your hands and ten fingers. Perhaps your hands are resting next to you or gently resting on your belly. (*Mention mudras only if your child practices them*).

Think about your mouth, your nose, your eyes. Relax them, letting the mouth fall open or stay closed, whichever is comfortable, and let the eyelids grow heavy and fall shut.

You feel completely relaxed, calm, and peaceful. You are safe. You are very loved.

Guided Meditation Story

Today you are at a giant sandpit. There is soft sand on the ground, as far as the eye can see. A few other children are also playing in this sandpit, as it is a lovely, warm, sunny day.

You settle down, plonking your bottom on the sand. You land with a soft thud. The sand laces in between your toes and tickles the bottoms of your bare feet. You drag your hands through the sand, tracing patterns with your fingers. You love the way the sand feels cool against your hands. It makes you feel calm.

There is a little brightblue bucket with a spade sitting close to you. You pick up the spade and plunge it into the sand, digging up more sand and throwing it into the blue bucket. You are going to build a sandcastle – a big one! With many rooms and a big moat around it. A princess will sit inside one of the towers, being guarded by a firebreathing dragon while her prince tries to save her.

As you are digging away, lost in your imagination, you see something gold glimmering in the sand. You move closer to take a better look. It appears to be a little golden chest sticking out of the sand. You use your

Story 17: The Magic Sandpit

spade to dig around the chest and, once it is loose, you pull it all the way out.

The chest is no bigger than the palm of your hand. The lid is encrusted with red jewels that sparkle in the sun. You use your fingers to pry open the lid. Inside the chest is a little piece of paper folded neatly in a square. You unfold the paper and smooth it out. The following instructions are written in black ink:

"If forwards is north and backward is south, if to the right is east, then where lies the west? Go that direction."

You think about it for a moment. The note mentions north is in front of you, south is behind you, east is to your right... so, to your left must be the west! You turn to your left and slowly walk, taking one step at a time. As you walk, you feel a sense of calm coming over you.

As you are about to take your tenth step, you see another folded piece of paper sticking out of the sand. You bend down to pick it up, unfolding it. Written in ink, again is a message:

'What goes up must come down."

What does that mean? you think as you look up into the sky. Floating down towards you is a tiny hotair balloon. The balloon is bright green and has a tiny wicker basket attached to it. The little hotair balloon lands gently on the sand, right in front of you.

You peer into the wicker basket. There is a small box inside. You lift the box out of the basket and open it. Inside is an even smaller hourglass – but there is no sand inside the hourglass, just a small, folded note.

You manage to screw the top of the hourglass off and take the note out. Written in ink is:

"Take a fistful of sand and fill me up with the sands of time. I am a reminder to you that even though time never stops, you can always live in the moment."

You smile. *What a nice idea.* You bend down to the sandpit and dig your fingers into the sand, collecting a fistful. You pour the sand into the hourglass and then screw the top back on. You turn the hourglass upside down and watch the sand quickly trickling to the bottom.

You spend the rest of the afternoon being mindful and enjoying the present moment. You build your sandcastle, creating four big towers with the bucket, and you dig a big, deep moat around the castle, pretending the moat is full of water. You imagine a beautiful princess with long flowing hair up in one of the towers. and a firebreathing green dragon guarding her tower while her prince rescues her.

When you are done playing, you decide to take a rest. Holding the hourglass in your hand, you lie back down in the sand and gaze up at the sky. There are some clouds that look like marshmallows floating by. The longer you stare at them, the more they start to look like animals. You can see a pig, a dog, and a cat.

You take in a deep breath, filling up your chest with air, and then breathe it all out, slowly. You notice how comfy your body feels, nestled into the sand. Your head, neck, shoulders, arms, fingers, belly, thighs, calves, feet, and toes feel heavy, as if they are melting into the sand.

In the distance, you can hear birds tweeting, as well as the soft rustle of the wind in the leaves of the trees. You take another deep breath in through your nose and as you breathe out, you can smell your favorite meal being cooked for you. It must be dinner time!

Slowly, you stand up, brushing the sand off your body. Clutching your hourglass in one hand, you head off back home, excited for dinner and thinking about the lovely day you had spending time by yourself, mindfully, living in the present moment, at the sandpit.

STORY 18
The Enchanting Garden

Getting Comfy

Settle into a cozy and comfortable position. Take a deep breath in, slowly filling up your lungs with air, and then let it all out with a sigh. Feel your body sinking deeper into the bed (*or couch*) and relax your head. If it feels good for you, close your eyes.

Simply listen to the sound of my voice and let your mind drift away.

Think about your little body, lying still and feeling warm. You can feel your chest rising and falling with each breath you take. Think about your feet and ten toes. Maybe your feet are falling out to the side. Maybe they are pointing straight up. However they are positioned is perfect.

Think about your hands and ten fingers. Perhaps your hands are resting next to you or gently resting on your belly. (*Mention mudras only if your child practices them*).

Think about your mouth, your nose, your eyes. Relax them, letting the mouth fall open or stay closed, whichever is comfortable, and let the eyelids grow heavy and fall shut.

You feel completely relaxed, calm, and peaceful. You are safe. You are very loved.

Guided Meditation Story

You find yourself in the middle of a most beautiful garden. Green ferns, plants, and trees surround you and butterflies gently float past from one flower to the next.

The air is cool and feels damp against your cheeks. You take a deep breath in, inhaling the rich smell of the garden. It smells like a mixture of soil, flowers, and freshness. This garden is so lovely, and you feel very happy to have found yourself here.

You slowly walk through the garden. On your right are bright red toadstools and on your left are tall bright-yellow sunflowers. As you continue to walk, following a little bushy path, you see a pair of wings up ahead. The wings are silver with gold spots and they look very delicate.

Attached to the wings is a little garden fairy! She turns around and sees you. "Oh, there you are!" she says.

You are a little confused. "Were you expecting me?" you ask her.

"Yes, I was! I need your help. But first, let me

Story 18: The Enchanting Garden

introduce myself, how rude of me! I am Fern, the Garden Fairy," she says.

"Hi, Fern. Nice to meet you. What do you need help with?" you ask.

"I have a beautiful little vegetable garden – well, I did have a beautiful little vegetable garden – until a big storm came and swept everything away!" Fern tells you.

"Oh, no! That's terrible," you say.

"Yes. But now I need help planting my vegetables again. Would you mind giving me a hand?" Fern asks.

You tell her you would love to help and that being outside in any sort of garden makes you feel very happy. You follow Fern back to her little cottage and she leads you out the back door.

"This is where my vegetable garden was," says Fern, pointing to a patch of dirt. Sitting next to the dirt patch are large wheelbarrows filled with all different types of vegetable plants and seeds.

"'Well!" you say, "let's get to work!".

Fern hands you a shovel and you start scooping up dirt, making neat rows in which to plant the new vegetables. You and Fern spend the rest of the afternoon planting pumpkins, cucumbers, tomatoes, carrots, and many more different types of vegetables.

As you plant the last carrot seedling, you notice the sun is starting to set. You stand up, wiping your dirt-covered hands against your pants. Grinning, you look over at Fern.

"I think our work here is done," you say.

"I think it is, too! I am so grateful for all your help today. Thank you so much. Please come back tomorrow, I have a surprise for you," says Fern.

You tell her you will return tomorrow, say goodbye, and make your way home. You sleep well that night, dreaming about garden fairies and dancing pumpkins and lettuce leaves!

The next day, you arrive back at Fern's cottage. You are very curious about her surprise. You knock on the front door.

"Around the back!" you hear Fern calling.

You walk around the side of her cottage and into the back garden. There, right before your eyes, is an amazing, rich, colorful vegetable garden. Fern is standing next to the vegetable garden with a watering can.

"What do you think?" asks Fern.

You cannot believe it. You can see red, plump, juicy tomatoes, brightgreen long cucumbers, crispy yellow peppers, orange crunchy carrots, and every single type of vegetable you can imagine.

"How did it all grow overnight!?" you ask Fern.

She smiles at you. "Magic," she says.

Fern hands you a basket and tells you to pick your favorite vegetables. You pluck some carrots, onions, garlic, red peppers, and potatoes from the garden.

"Let's go inside – and bring your basket, I am going to make you the best fairy vegetable soup you have ever had!" she says.

Story 18: The Enchanting Garden

"This will be the first fairy vegetable soup I have ever had!" you tell Fern. She giggles.

In the kitchen, Fern gets to work, flapping her wings quickly as she cooks. You watch her from the kitchen table, noticing the delicious aromas starting to waft out of the pot. When the soup is ready, she uses a big ladle to scoop the soup into a big bowl. Fern floats over to the table and places a big steaming bowl down in front of you.

You take a sip of the broth – delicious! It warms your throat and chest and feels like velvet.

"This is so yummy!" you tell Fern.

Fern smiles. "Because this is fairy vegetable soup, you will start to notice how relaxed you feel as you eat it," she says.

You finish the bowl of soup and as you set your spoon down, you feel a deep, lovely feeling washing over you. Your body feels extremely relaxed and you are starting to feel sleepy. Your legs and arms feel heavy and you would love to curl up and fall asleep.

Fern notices you becoming drowsy and flutters over to you, scoops you up in her arms, and glides out the door. She flies you through the big garden and all the way back to your house. She places you gently in your bed, says goodnight, and flies away.

You are grateful to be in your bed. Snuggling down into your blanket and pillows, you close your eyes and fall into a deep and delicious sleep.

STORY 19
Camping in the Wild

Getting Comfy

Settle into a cozy and comfortable position. Take a deep breath in, slowly filling up your lungs with air, and then let it all out with a sigh. Feel your body sinking deeper into the bed (*or couch*) and relax your head. If it feels good for you, close your eyes.

Simply listen to the sound of my voice and let your mind drift away.

Think about your little body, lying still and feeling warm. You can feel your chest rising and falling with each breath you take. Think about your feet and ten toes. Maybe your feet are falling out to the side. Maybe they are pointing straight up. However they are positioned is perfect.

Think about your hands and ten fingers. Perhaps your hands are resting next to you or gently resting on your belly. (*Mention mudras only if your child practices them*).

Think about your mouth, your nose, your eyes. Relax them, letting the mouth fall open or stay closed, whichever is comfortable, and let the eyelids grow heavy and fall shut.

You feel completely relaxed, calm, and peaceful. You are safe. You are very loved.

Guided Meditation Story

You are in the car with your family on the way to go camping. You are so excited! You love camping; setting up the tent, sitting around a campfire, roasting marshmallows, gazing up at the starry sky.

When you arrive, you jump out of the car and take in your surroundings. The air is fresh, and the temperature is just right. Your family chooses a grassy clearing in between a few tall trees to set up the tent. The spot is perfect. You help carry firewood, coolers filled with fresh food, and camping equipment from the car to the camping spot.

Once everything is set up, you plonk down into a camping chair and take a deep breath in and out. In the distance, you can hear the sound of trickling water. You stand up and follow the sound. It leads you to a creek. The water is crystal clear, and you can see pebbles at the bottom. You slowly wade into the water, feeling the wetness on your feet.

The water is cool and refreshing. You bend down and cup your hands, filling them with water and splashing it on your face. Ahhh! That feels nice. You tilt your head back and look up at the sky. The sky is turning a

Story 19: Camping in the Wild

purplered color as the sun is starting to set. This is your favorite time of the day when you are camping! The fire can be lit and the campfire storytelling can begin!

You head back to the campsite and take your seat by the fire. Dinner is being cooked over the fire and it smells delicious. As the sun disappears completely, it starts to get a bit cooler, so you bring your chair a little closer to the fire. The flames are red and orange, dancing in front of you.

Once you have eaten dinner, your family takes it in turns to tell stories. As you listen, you watch the flames of the fire and feel yourself getting sleepy. Very slowly, you start to nod off, closing your eyes, and feeling the warmth of the fire on your face.

When you wake up, you find yourself snuggled in your sleeping bag inside your tent. You must have fallen asleep at the campfire and been put to bed. You listen, but it is quiet, which means your family must have gone to bed, too. You lie there, feeling happy that you are camping tonight and thinking how nice it would be to watch the stars.

You crawl out of your sleeping bag and put on a jumper before you unzip your tent and head outside. Your camping chair is still set up, so you go and sit in it and look up at the stars. The sky is black, and the stars are shining brightly. You can see a cluster of stars close together and if you look at it for long enough, it looks like the shape of a dog!

Suddenly, from behind you, you hear a noise. You

spin around. A cute little dragon is standing there, waving at you!

"Hello! Don't be afraid. I am Calvin The Camping Dragon. I visit all children when they are camping," says Calvin.

"Oh, hello! You startled me," you tell Calvin.

"I know, I'm sorry. I never know quite how to introduce myself. Because I am a dragon, people automatically fear me, so I guess I have just gotten used to sneaking up on people," he says.

"That's ok, Calvin. I'm not scared of you; you're a cute little dragon! You are only the size of my foot," you tell him.

"Exactly!" says Calvin with a smile.

He walks over to you and stands at the edge of the burnt firewood where the fire had been earlier that evening. He takes a deep breath in and when he breathes out, fire comes out of his nose and onto the wood, which ignites the campfire.

"Wow!" you say. "That is so cool!"

"It is a little trick of mine," says Calvin as he sits down next to you and stretches his arms out in front of him, warming his hands over the flames.

Calvin The Camping Dragon looks up at you. "Would you like to do some meditation with me?" he asks you.

You tell him you would love that but that it might make you sleepy, and if it does, you will head back into your tent and go to bed. He says that is fine.

Story 19: Camping in the Wild

"Close your eyes," says Calvin. "Learning to meditate is one of the best tools you will ever have. It can calm you down anywhere, anytime, and once you become really good at it, it becomes a lot easier."

You nod, keeping your eyes closed.

"Start by dropping your shoulders away from your ears and making sure your teeth aren't clenched together. Sink into your chair and try to completely relax your body so you aren't holding tension anywhere," instructs Calvin.

You drop your shoulders and part your lips, allowing your tongue to rest gently in your mouth.

"Now, try and picture your mind as empty. The point of meditation is to stop paying attention to your thoughts and simply make space for nothing – for not thinking. Which is a lot harder to do than it sounds!" laughs Calvin.

"I want you to choose a special word. You will repeat this word to yourself over and over again in your mind. When a thought comes into your mind, accept that it is there and then simply turn your attention back to your word, repeating it. What word do you want to choose?" asks Calvin.

"I am going to choose the word *love*, Calvin," you tell him.

"That is a perfect word. Try and empty your mind of thoughts and just focus on the word *love*. Remember, it is perfectly okay and normal for thoughts to come to your mind. Perhaps you think about your dog or your friends or your teacher. Accept the thought and then think about the word *love* again."

For a few minutes, you and Calvin sit in silence, side by side, meditating. You feel calm and safe as you focus on the word *love*. After a while, you can feel yourself becoming sleepy again. You open your eyes and turn to look at Calvin, who has his eyes closed and looks like he is in a deep meditative state.

"Calvin?" you say. Calvin keeps his eyes closed. "Calvin," you say again, this time a little louder. Calvin opens his eyes.

"Yes, sorry! I have been practicing meditation for so many years that now when I meditate, I really meditate, and I am so focused I don't hear anything else around me," he says.

"No worries. I hope I get to that stage one day. For now, I am going to go back to my tent and go to bed."

"Of course! It was nice to meet you and I am glad you learned about the beauty of meditation tonight," says Calvin.

You say goodnight and head back into your tent, snuggling down into your sleeping bag. You close your eyes and notice how calm and relaxed you feel. Falling asleep will be easy tonight and you cannot wait to practice meditation tomorrow.

STORY 20
Superhero Party

Getting Comfy

Settle into a cozy and comfortable position. Take a deep breath in, slowly filling up your lungs with air, and then let it all out with a sigh. Feel your body sinking deeper into the bed (*or couch*) and relax your head. If it feels good for you, close your eyes.

Simply listen to the sound of my voice and let your mind drift away.

Think about your little body, lying still and feeling warm. You can feel your chest rising and falling with each breath you take. Think about your feet and ten toes. Maybe your feet are falling out to the side. Maybe they are pointing straight up. However they are positioned is perfect.

Think about your hands and ten fingers. Perhaps your hands are resting next to you or gently resting on your belly. (*Mention mudras only if your child practices them*).

Think about your mouth, your nose, your eyes. Relax them, letting the mouth fall open or stay closed, whichever is comfortable, and let the eyelids grow heavy and fall shut.

You feel completely relaxed, calm, and peaceful. You are safe. You are very loved.

Guided Meditation Story

You wake up this morning with extra pep in your step! You are very excited; it's your best friend's birthday party, and the theme is superheroes!

You jump out of bed and head to your closet where your superhero outfit is hanging up. You open the closet door and see your outfit. It is super cool – a bright red bodysuit with a big, flowy, green cape. You take your costume out and put it on, spinning around your bedroom. You love how your cape swishes behind you.

In the car on the way to the party, you chat with your mom about how excited you are about the party. You wonder what kind of food you will eat, what games you will play, and if you will receive a party bag at the end.

You arrive at your friend's house and knock on the door. Your friend opens the door to greet you. He is also wearing a cape, but his cape is bright yellow. He invites you inside and you join the rest of the kids out in the garden. Everyone is dressed up as superheroes and they all look great!

You notice a table filled with different snacks and treats. You wander over to have a look. There is a big

Story 20: Superhero Party

plate piled high with superhero cookies, bowls filled with little chocolate cakes, and sliced bread dotted with dark chocolate sprinkles. You pick up a cookie and take a bite. It is sweet and buttery and tastes delicious.

Your friend's mom announces that a game of hideandseek will start. You love hideandseek, and always find the best hiding spots. Your best friend covers his eyes with his hands and starts slowly counting while you all run off to find a spot to hide.

You run down the back of the garden where you see a big oak tree. The tree has lots of branches, making it easy for you to climb. You climb up to a branch and nestle into the side of the tree trunk. There are green leaves all around you; it is the perfect hiding spot.

You glance around you; none of the other children have found this tree, so they must be hiding in other spots around the house. You sit patiently, waiting for your best friend to stop counting and start his search.

"Pssst!" you hear behind you.

You turn around to see who is making the sound.

"Pssst! Over here!" says the voice.

You look harder and in the tree behind you, perched up in the branches, is another superhero. Except this superhero is an adult, not a child.

"Were you also invited to the party, and are you hiding in this tree, too?" you ask her.

"What party?" she asks.

You are confused.

"It is my best friend's birthday today and he is holding a superheroes party," you say.

"Oh! How funny! No, no, I am not here for the party. I climbed up here to rescue a cat that was stuck in the branches. I rescued him, but now I am sort of stuck myself," says the woman, looking a little sheepish.

"Then why are you dressed as a superhero?" you ask her.

"Oh! I *am* a superhero".

Your eyes grow wide.

"A *real* superhero?" you ask her.

"Yes. My name is Sassy the Superhero! Nice to meet you. I would shake your hand if I could, but I don't want to let go of this branch," says Sassy.

"Wow! I can't believe I am meeting a reallife superhero," you say.

"Well, usually I am not stuck up in trees, but this is a big tree!"

You climb over from your branch to the trunk of the tree and look up at the limb that Sassy is stuck on. She is up pretty high.

"Sassy, can you use your cape to help you jump down?" you ask her.

"Oh! That is a good idea! I always forget about my cape and how it helps me to fly."

Sassy uses one of her hands to flap her cape around and suddenly a golden light surrounds her, and she gently floats back down to the ground.

"Thanks!" says Sassy.

Story 20: Superhero Party

'You're welcome. I wish I had a real superhero cape," you tell her.

"Well. As a real superhero, I have the power to turn your cape into a superhero cape," says Sassy.

She walks towards you and points at your cape.

"By the power invested in me, I hereby turn your costume cape into a real superhero cape!".

A golden glow surrounds your cape, and, after a moment, your cape begins to sparkle.

"There you go!" says Sassy.

"Wow! Thanks, Sassy! What can I do with my cape?" you ask.

"Well, besides being able to fly with it, us superheroes usually use our capes to switch on our one special superpower. Each superhero has one power. Mine is meditation. I can close my eyes and instantly, I calm down and switch into meditate mode. What's yours?" asks Sassy.

"Mine is…being able to relax instantly when I click my fingers," you tell Sassy.

"That is a fabulous superpower!" says Sassy. "Let's practice them now."

Sassy sits down on the ground, crosses her legs, and closes her eyes. She falls deep into a meditative state. She looks so peaceful in her superhero outfit and cape.

You click your fingers, and as soon as you do you feel a calming feeling sweep over your body. Starting from the very top of your head, a warm glow starts to wind its way down to your throat, your chest, your arms, hands and fingers, your tummy, your thighs, legs, feet and toes.

You are both amazed and delighted at how good you feel. You also feel lucky that you have this new skill as you realize you can click your fingers whenever and wherever and instantly feel relaxed. What an amazing skill to have!

Sassy is still meditating. You notice her index fingers are touching her thumbs while her other three fingers are straight. You wonder what she is doing.

Slowly, she opens her eyes and smiles at you.

"Ahh, I feel so relaxed. I always do after I meditate, it really relaxes my entire body and mind," says Sassy.

"What symbol were you making with your hands?" you ask her.

"That is called a *mudra*. They are different symbols you make with your hands. There are many mudras you can do; they allow the energy to flow through your body to different points. That particular mudra is called the 'Gyan'. It is a popular mudra to do while you are meditating," Sassy says.

"That is so cool! I would love to learn more about meditation and mudras. Now that I have this amazing superpower of instantly relaxing with a click of my fingers, I think meditation would also be a great tool for me to learn," you say.

"Yes!" says Sassy. "I will teach you some time."

In the distance, you hear your name being called. Your best friend has come to look for you. Oops! You

Story 20: Superhero Party

completely forgot about hideandseek. You turn back to Sassy.

"It was lovely to meet you Sassy, but I must be getting back to the party. I am supposed to be hiding, we are playing hideandseek," you tell her.

"Of course! Lovely meeting you, too, and soon enough I will come and find you so I can teach you some simple meditation tricks. Take care!" says Sassy.

With a swoosh of her cape, she is gone.

You quickly run behind a tree, peeking around the trunk. Your best friend is getting closer.

"I'm coming! Where are you?" he calls.

You can't help but let out a giggle. Your friend hears you and runs over towards the tree.

"Gotcha!" he yells as he finds you. The two of you laugh and make your way back to the party.

At the end of the afternoon, as the birthday party is coming to an end, your friend hands out party bags to everyone. You open yours and have a look. Inside is a superhero mask, a couple of yummy sweets, and a tiny book no bigger than the palm of your hand. It has a blank cover. You open it up and written on the inside of the cover, it says:

"It was so nice to meet you today. I have never met such a young, mindful superhero before. Here is a list of mudras and some easy tips to get started with meditation. Have a read and when you are finished, I will find you and we will practice meditating together. Love, Sassy."

You smile and wonder how Sassy knew which party

bag was yours. However, you weren't surprised; she is a superhero, after all.

Your mom picks you up and takes you home. Later that night, as you are snuggled up in your bed, underneath the blankets with your pillows, you have a little look through your special meditation book from Sassy. You are fascinated by all the mudras and how it works.

When you feel yourself getting sleepy, you put your book down beside your bed and curl up. You are tired from the day, but you also feel so peaceful that you drift off into a deep sleep and don't wake up until the morning.

Conclusion

Now that you have grasped the basics of mindfulness and meditation with these stories, we encourage you to continue to find moments to be mindful on a daily basis. Mindfulness and meditation take practice. It doesn't just happen overnight, but rather over a period of time. If you practice even 25 minutes of mindfulness each day, it will be easier for you to switch your busy mind into a mindful mode. Below are some tips on how to incorporate mindful habits into your everyday life: (to be read by the child or the parent)

- When you wake up in the morning, think about what the purpose of your day is going to be. Are you going to work really hard at school and finish all your class exercises on time? Are you going to do something nice for a friend today? Are you going to try and smile all day? Or are you simply going to have a good day? Pick one aim for the day and stick with it.
- In general, most of us eat too quickly. Rarely do we take the time to really focus on what we are eating – how it tastes, how it smells, what

it feels like to chew. When you eat your food, take a few deep breaths before beginning to eat. As you chew your food, think about how much you are enjoying the food. As you continue your meal, think about whether you are starting to feel full, and if you do feel full, feel free to stop eating because that is your body telling you it has had enough.

- Aim to move your body a little each day. Perhaps playing basketball or soccer, or swimming in the pool, is your favorite activity, or maybe you enjoy walks outside. Whatever it is, even if it's just playing outside with your dog, try and do it every day. As you are moving, simply notice the sensations you feel. Take note of how it makes you feel. Moving your body and getting the blood flowing helps foster a healthy mind.

- Take a couple of minutes each day to sit down with a friend, family member, or teacher to observe and recognize feelings you are having in your body. Perhaps your chest feels warm and you feel light and happy. Maybe on another day, you feel angry and your head feels hot. Talking about how you feel is a great way to practice mindfulness.

- Walking slowly through nature is a fantastic way to connect with the earth. It enables you to take in your surroundings – the smells, noises, sights, and sounds. Perhaps you can quietly point out all the things you see along your walk.

- If you find yourself feeling overwhelmed or nervous, take a few moments to practice deep belly breaths. Place your hand on your belly and take a deep, slow breath in through your nose; then breathe out, again through your nose, slowly. Visualize blowing up a balloon full of air and then releasing the air. Take five of these deep belly breaths.
- At the end of the day, before you go to sleep, either write down or tell someone three things for which you are grateful. Maybe you are grateful for the wonderful friends you have, your puppy, and your birthday coming up soon. Or perhaps the sun shone brightly that day, you ate your favorite foods, and you won a spelling competition.
- Sometimes you can simply stop what you are doing and observe. Notice what is going on around you and engage your five senses – smell, touch, sight, hearing, and taste.
- We sincerely hope you (and your child) have enjoyed these mindful and meditation stories. Learning how to switch off a busy mind and turn to a mindful mode is a powerful tool, one that will be useful for the rest of one's life. Our hope is that these stories encourage you to dive deeper into the world of mindfulness and meditation, as there is so much to learn and explore.

May I ask you a small favor?

If you enjoyed this book and got helpful pointers and actionable strategies from it, **would you consider letting others know about it?**

Here are several ways you can do so:

#1 Leave a review on Amazon
#2 Leave a review at Goodreads
#3 Tell your peeps about it on your **Blog, Podcast,** or **YouTube** Channel
#4 Share it on **Facebook, Instagram, Twitter, Pinterest,** or **LinkedIn**
#5 Mention it to your **friends and family members,** or your colleagues at work

Reviews on Amazon are incredibly helpful both for other readers to decide whether this book will be useful to them and for indie authors and publishers to get the word out about our books. Your support is much appreciated!

Thanks in advance for your good deeds!

You are a STAR...:)

Warm regards,

Ava Johansson

YOUR FREE BONUS
The Beginners Guide to Mudras for Kids!

As a way of thanking you for your purchase, I have a **free bonus** to offer you.

Besides the beautiful meditation and bedtime stories provided in this book, I have created **The Beginners Guide to Mudras for Kids,** which will teach your kids the hand symbols they can use during a guided meditation story. The guide explains why mudras are beneficial and what it all means. Your kids will master the main mudras in no time.

Click (or tap) below to get your FREE Bonus instantly.

Click here:
https://www.mangobroom.com/mudras-kids/

References

Headspace., 2018. Meditation 101. What Is Meditation?

Yoga International., 2019. The Real Meaning of Meditation.

New Horizon Holistic Centre, 2017. Kids Meditation.

Ten Percent Blog., 2018. What's The Difference Between Meditation and Mindfulness?

Parents., 2020. Why Sleep Meditation Works for Kids and How to Try It.

Hello Lunch Lady., 2019. Bedtime Meditation Kids.

Thrive Global., 2019. The Benefits of Meditation for Kids.

Green Children Magazine., 2021. Free Meditation Guided Relaxation Scripts.

The Inspired Tree House., 2017. Calming Breathing Techniques Kids.

Mindful Child Aerial Yoga., 2018. Mudras Yoga for Little Hands.

Chopra., 2021. 10 Powerful Mudras and How to Use Them.

The New York Times Guides., 2017. Mindfulness For Children.

Printed in Poland
by Amazon Fulfillment
Poland Sp. z o.o., Wrocław